Janey Mack
Me Shirt is Black

First published 1982
The O'Brien Press Ltd.
20 Victoria Road Dublin 6.

British Library Cataloguing in Publication Data
MacThomáis, Éamonn
    Janey Mack, me shirt is black.
    1. Folklore, Irish   2. Streets — Folklore.
    I. Title
    398'.355   GR153.5

    ISBN 0-905140-67-2

The publishers would like to thank
Muriel McCarthy and M. Paul Pollard for their
help with this book.

Typesetting: Redsetter Ltd.
Origination: Trish McAdam
Book Design: Michael O'Brien
Jacket Design: Jarlath Hayes
Binding: John F. Newman
Printed in the Republic of Ireland
by Irish Elsevier Printers

Janey Mack
Me Shirt is Black

Éamonn Mac Thomáis

THE O'BRIEN PRESS

DUBLIN

Other books by Éamonn Mac Thomáis

Me Jewel and Darlin' Dublin
Gur Cake and Coal Blocks
The Labour and The Royal

Contents

For Orla, Shane, Meliosa and Damien

Bang Bang (Lord Dudley) and Éamonn Mac Thomáis

1

The Ha'penny Bridge

THERE WAS A TIME when a new shop opened every Sunday at the Ha'penny Bridge. They all gave twelve months guarantees with clocks, watches and radios. The following week they were gone like winter's snow. 'Five years, I'm giving, only for this week, five years guarantee with all my clocks and watches,' said the little dealer working out of a brown attaché case. 'Five years,' said an old fella. 'He'll be gone in five minutes if he sells that junk.'

Years and years ago, there was only three shops on the Ha'penny Bridge. The first shop was run by Hector Grey who started the tradition of Sunday selling at the Ha'penny Bridge. Hector's claim to fame and success lay in the fact that he sold quality goods at workmen's prices. The second shop was run by Paddy Slattery. Paddy sold among other things, glass and tile cutters. He must have taught half of Dublin to cut glass. His demonstration of glass cutting was better than the Theatre Royal. Paddy's a Limerick man who went to Cork city as a child and went to school with the famous Frank O'Connor. The first thing I bought off Paddy, forty years ago, was a card of twelve brass tie pins for a shilling. The same tie pins sold in the shops at sixpence each. In those years a man or youth wouldn't be caught dead without a tie pin. The third shop was a book cart, and Joe Clarke was the book seller. He was famous for having a powerful selection of books and if you didn't see anything

Buy Away, Buy Away,

New Shop Open,
Hams, Jams and anything
You want, Mam.

on the cart to fancy, you were invited down to his book warehouse in Strand Street. Once a month Joe had a special sale of new magazines. 'Five for a shilling, *Red Letter, The Oracle, Picture Post, Woman's Way* and *Woman's Weekly.*'

With the exception of *Picture Post,* the other magazines were women's only. So Joe must have been the first man in Dublin to raise the Women's Lib. Flag. 'Don't forget the wife, the mother, the granny, the girl friend, or the sister, a man should be good to his sister. Buy five for a shilling or ten for two bob.' They sold like hot cross buns on a Good Friday.

Hector called it the Metal Bridge. 'Metal Bridge prices, gentlemen.' Joe called it the Iron Bridge. 'Iron Bridge Books or my warehouse in Strand Street or the Carlisle Bridge on Saturdays. All prices marked inside the covers. Where would you get the *Life of Lord Edward Fitzgerald* for eightpence or bibles for a bob?' 'Are these Catholic or Protestant bibles?' a man asked. 'They're God's bibles, sir,' said Joe, 'and I think He was a Jew.' The late Seamus O'Sullivan, poet and prose writer, well his father was buying books at the Ha'penny Bridge. 'How much is this bible?' he asked. 'A half crown, sir.' 'But it's marked one shilling inside the cover,' he replied. 'I'm surprised at such a l'arned gentleman underestimatin' the value of the word of God' said Joe. Old Joe and the book cart are long gone, but at the time of writing Hector and Paddy are still going strong with no thoughts of retirement, after fifty-one years of selling.

A great boom came to the Ha'penny Bridge selling five years ago. Tony McMahon, a Limerick man, and Dave McGuinness, a Dublin man, who started street selling in Thomas Street in the Liberties on a Saturday, opened a shop at the Ha'penny Bridge. The selling, the crack, the good manners, the friendliness and 'bring it back next week if you are not satisfied,' is one of the joys of Dublin. 'The "Limdub" Shop,' in Joyce's words, is under the canopy of the Dublin Woollen Company Shop, while Hector is out in all weather with his back to the Irish Woollen Company Shop. Hector doesn't seem to mind; when it rains he sells umbrellas, when the sun shines he sells sun-glasses.

The Dublin Woollen Company was established in the year 1888. For years it had a big notice-board with these words written on it: 'This Shop has no connection with the Shop next door'. Paddy Slattery always sold with his back to this sign. On the far side of the Ha'penny Bridge is the Irish Woollen Mills. This quarter of Dublin has been famous for woollens, tweeds, buttons, His Master's Voice records, old furniture, antiques, opticians, coin shops, picture framers, books and McGrath's Tea. The tea is gone for its tea now and so is McGrath's building. Another regular pair of sellers at the Ha'penny Bridge were Paddy and Christina Rice. Two real Dubs, with wit at their fingertips and bargains at their stall. Now that they have gone all swanky with their shop and stall in Thomas Street, they take Sunday off. The sweet man is Tom Kelly, who sells bullseyes by the ton. Joe Fitzpatrick is the artist who sits in the film director's chair looking like a young Van Gogh, and adding colour and glamour to the ol' Ha'penny Bridge. The customers every Sunday are all friends, wits and characters. I can't name them all but I'll be kilt' if I don't mention Pat Thomas, Steve Clery, who says he's not related to the O'Connell Street Clerys, Paddy Palles, Sean Higgins. Some day us five are going to hire out a juggernaut and bring back to the Ha'penny Bridge all the nick-nacks, treasures, bargains, junk, rubbish and bric-a-brac that we bought down the years and auction it off to the highest bidder, and we'll hire the 'Limdub' sales manager, Frances Delaney, to do the selling.

On Saturday afternoons, the Ha'penny Bridge was reserved for side shows and mini carnivals. Blondini the Sword Swallower, Houdini who got himself tied up with a straight jacket and nearly burst his eyes getting out of it. The Cart Wheel man who balanced a heavy cart wheel on his chin and then lay on broken bottles for an encore. The Whip man who whipped cigarettes out of his wife's mouth. The wife used to look at him as if she was saying, 'If you miss I'll brain ye'. When the act was over, him and the wife used to smoke all the half cigarettes. But the wife held on to the money that was thrown into the ring.

11

The Magic Soap man was one of the best acts at the Ha'penny Bridge. He stood on a butter box selling Magic Soap. 'The Magic Soap only needs a drop of water, it's for cleaning suits,' he'd say. He'd pick a kid with a dirty scruffy suit, then he'd wet his Magic Soap with a few drops of water out of a baby Power bottle. The wet soap was rubbed up and down the lapel, in next to no time the lapel looked like new. The faces of the kids looking at the brand new bit of the scruffy suit! 'Mister, do the trousers, ah go wan, mister, do the trousers.' This was in the era of expensive dry cleaning and the Magic Soap bars sold very well for a shilling.

'Grain the Hall Door, Mam,' was another great act. The Grain Man had a little board of wood, two steel combs and a ball of cotton wool. He used to show how easy it was to grain a hall door. His hands worked like lightning as he grained board, design after design, oak, mahogany, hazel nut, walnut or French polish. He did the French polish act on the other side of the board. His Grain Set sold for two shillings. All Dublin was out with the two little steel combs and balls of cotton wool. Some hall doors looked beautiful, others looked like coffins and piebald ponies.

Blind men, musicians, singers, beggars and holy picture sellers all made the Ha'penny Bridge their own. The winos used to like sitting where the man sat in olden times collecting the ha'pennies. The Iron Bridge, as the Corpo' called it in their reports, was a toll bridge. It cost a ha'penny to cross and two men were employed to collect the ha'pennies. The bridge opened from sunrise to sunset. One day I was crossing the Ha'penny Bridge when a beggar man stuck out his hand. 'How much? ' I asked. 'Give us two bob,' he said. 'Two bob,' said I, 'and me mother only paid a ha'penny.' 'Ah yes,' said the beggar man. 'But in those times the ha'penny was 'subsided' by the British Government.' After he got his two bob he went on to tell me that he liked working at the Ha'penny Bridge. 'Just think, the amount of good that I'm helping people to do.'

Well, Willie Walsh and Johnny Claudius Beresford weren't thinking of the good they were going to do when they got

12

the idea of building the Iron Bridge. 'Pots of money and no work,' said Johnny. Willie was a ferry man on the Liffey. In fact he owned the seven ferries that toured the Liffey daily bringing people back and forth. Johnny was a man of many trades. He was lord mayor, toll collector, revenue commissioner, alderman, jailer and executioner of United Irishmen. Willie had the contract for seven years to supply the Liffey with ferries, provided that he spent one thousand pounds to repair his leaky ferries. In the year 1814 Willie asked the Corpo' for half a year's rent back as there was no business on the Liffey. Willie and Johnny got drinking one night and began making the poor mouth to one another. 'Lookit,' said Johnny, 'I brought over James Gandon to build the Custom House, the Four Courts, the King's Inns and many more. I saved them from the Rebellion in '98 and the thanks I got was to be asked to surrender the toll charges.' 'Willie,' said he, 'how would you like to build a bridge, sell your ferries and sit at home and rake in the ha'pence? ' Willie was all ears. Before they left the Eagle Tavern, the partnership was agreed.

The next morning they both went to the Ballast Board and asked for two pieces of the Liffey River. The Ballast Board was delighted with Willie and Johnny's plans and gave them the Liffey water scot free. The next move was made by Willie. He asked the Corpo' for another lease on the Liffey for thirty-one years. The Corpo' gave the lease and then they were asked for permission to build the bridge. In two years the bridge went up. The Iron Bridge for the Iron Duke and ha'pennies for Willie and Johnny. The official opening was held in 1816 and it was named 'Wellington Bridge'. Another lease was given to Johnnie and Willie for seventy years. After that time the Corpo' was to take over control of the Iron Bridge. But another lease was got and the Corpo' had to wait until 29th September 1917 to stop the ha'penny charge. The bridge cost £3,894, seven shillings and elevenpence ha'penny. Now you can work out for yourself how many people Willie and Johnny needed to make a good weekly profit and don't forget to allow for the two gatemen who collected the ha'pennies and each were paid two shillings and fourpence a week. The rent of the bridge was £353 a year, in old currency, including the run of seven ferries all along the Liffey.

Most people rush across the Ha'penny Bridge. I like to stroll slowly, watching the blue and white skyline over Liffey Street and Bachelor's Walk. I like to listen to the sound of the auctioneers' bell and admire the three bridge lamps. Sometimes I stand in the middle of the bridge and look west up the River Liffey counting the green domes, Adam and Eve's, Moses and Patrick, Peter and Paul, then I turn eastwards and look down the river at Liberty Hall, Loopline, Hibernia Commerce and Conciliation Hall. A special look is given to George Webb's book shops. How I love to linger at the outside book stalls where the Fenian, John O'Leary, browsed through the leather-bound volumes. O'Leary had ten thousand books in his library. The pavements here are lined with the footprints of all the great patriots and literary men of Dublin: Pearse, Connolly, Plunkett, MacDonagh, Joyce, Synge, Yeats, O'Casey, Shaw, Stephens and Seamus O'Sullivan. A walk through Merchants' Arch brings to mind memories of Thomas Traynor and the Ouzel Galley. Traynor had a shoemaker's shop in Merchants' Arch. He fought in the Easter Week Rising 1916 and was executed by the British during the Black and Tan War. There is a fine memorial to him in Tullow, County Carlow. Commercial Buildings and the old Ouzel Galley are gone and are now replaced by the Central Bank. When the Central Bank went up to its full height I always thought it looked like Napoleon's hat, looking down on Wellington's Ha'penny Bridge, a little poetic justice, him getting his own back for Waterloo. But planning permission saved Wellington embarrassment. The hat was cut off by Corpo' orders.

In the year 1695 the *Ouzel* galley left Ringsend bound for the eastern seas. With Captain Eoghan Massey in command she was due back in Dublin in twelve months. A year passed, no sign of the *Ouzel,* another year and yet another year still no sign of the galley. The owners, Messrs. Ferris, Twigg and Cash, claimed the insurance, and after a bit of hassle the insurance was paid in full. The galley was lost and the Ringsend sailors with her. Five years after the day she sailed the shouts and roars came up the Liffey, 'The Ouzel is back, Massey has brought her home.' It was no rumour, it was God's truth. The *Ouzel* galley sailed into Dublin's port. What a story Captain Massey and the Ringsend sailors had. Captured by pirates, he escaped and took the ship from the pirates and sailed home. Robinson Crusoe was only in the ha'penny place. The ship was still laden with her own cargo and all the pirate's gold and booty. Now the fun started. Who owned the ship and its cargo? The shippers had been paid, so they didn't own it. The insurance could not claim it as they had contracted to insure it, so who owned the *Ouzel* galley?

The Corpo' members were in knots, the shippers were in knots, the insurance were in knots. After many's the hot and cold words spoken, it was agreed that the *Ouzel* galley and its cargo would provide a fund to alleviate poverty amongst the merchants of Dublin. The merchants in turn decided to band themselves together for the settlement of commercial disputes and to divvy out the charitable funds. The Ouzel Galley Society was founded in the year 1705. They held their early meetings in the Rose and Bottle Tavern in Dame Street. Today's Dublin Chamber of Commerce takes their foundation year from the old Ouzel Galley. The last act before the Ouzel Galley Society folded up in 1888 was to donate funds to six Dublin hospitals. The next time you cross the Ha'penny Bridge, look down at the Liffey water and if the tide is coming in, remember that's the same tide that brought in the *Ouzel* galley after the bit of a scrap with the pirates.

2

Youngfellas, Here's Youngwans

I SWEAR BY THE stain — the stain is the yoke that the Vikings swore on at College Green in days gone by — that I never in all my days gave any youngwan apples, pears or sixpence to kiss her. Sure kisses were always ten a penny. In fact, they weren't even a penny. A kiss could be got in the woodeners in the Tivo or Inchicore or Fountain Picture House for a few bullseyes, a piece of orange, a bite out of your apple or a suck of your ice-cream wafer. And of course kisses were stolen when the lights went out and the youngwans would never know who did it. Now and again the silence in the picture house would be broken by a youngwan's voice crying out, 'Johnny, take your hand off me knee. Here's your Woodbine back.'

Now there was no love at eleven years of age in our day. No, I think I was twelve when I began to notice meself going home from school the long way round by Goldenbridge Convent. I also remember rushing up and down to the Liberties for bread and the other messages so that I'd have time before tea to turn the skipping rope for the girls. Suddenly I began to love skipping and had no time for football or boxing the fox. The skipping rhymes made us feel important, wanted and grown up.

Johnny gave me apples,
Johnny gave me pears,
Johnny gave me sixpence
To kiss him on the stairs.
I gave him back his apples
I gave him back his pears
I gave him back his sixpence
And threw him down the stairs.
He fell into a lake,
And swallowed a snake,
And he came back up
With a bad belly ache.

He is handsome,
He is pretty,
He is a boy from Dublin city.
He is courting
One two three,
Oh! please tell me
Who is he?

Eamonn Thomas said he loves her,
All the boys are fighting for her.
He knocks up the knocker,
He picks up a pin,
And he asks Mrs. Dillon, is her daughter in?
She's neither in
And she's neither out
But she's down in the garden walking about.
Up comes Winnie all dressed in white,
A rose in her petticoat
And a small can of milk.
Oh! says Winnie will you have a sup of this?
No, says Eamonn I'd rather have a kiss.
He brings her down to the garden,
And he sits her on his knee.
And he says, now Winnie
Will you marry me?
Yes — No,
Certainly so.

And the rope would be turned quicker and quicker, but I always managed to give it a jerk at the 'certainly so' part of the song.

The trouble at twelve years of age was making up one's mind as to which girl was the nicest. There were only hundreds of them coming out of Goldenbridge Convent, and the pigtails which we used to pull and think looked horrible, now began to look cute. Clicking mots became our favourite pastime. The best place for making eyes was turning the skipping rope, until some little youngwan brought us back to childhood by singing the rhyme 'Teddy Bear'.

Teddy bear teddy bear
Tip your toe.

We always chanted back,

Teddy bear teddy bear
On the poe.

We threw down the rope and ran away, leaving the girls shocked that we uttered such a word as poe.

As the days rolled by we found skipping to be only a child's game and there was more fun to be got at Griffith Bridge on the Grand Canal watching all the youngwans coming from work in Polikoff's Factory. Sometimes we'd get up enough courage to shout across the canal's green waters, 'Youngwans here's youngfellas,' and sometimes they shouted back, 'Come on over here, youngfellas here's youngwans.' But we never dared go across to the other side. Then someone suggested that Kilmainham Cross was a better place for clicking mots as you had the youngwans from Fullers, Rowntrees and Dunlop's Laundry. The blonde outa Fullers was only massive, she was like a film star. Then someone said, 'Do yeh know the one in the green coat outa the Dunlop's Laundry? Well she lives in Bluebell, me brother knows her.' We glared at him. How dare his brother know our girlfriend when our girlfriend didn't even know she was being admired and loved from Swift's orchard at Kilmainham Cross. Mots, birds, bits of fluff, lovely Janes, and will you look at your wan outa Rowntrees, she's a sight for sore eyes.

One of the best ways for clicking mots was the mot's bike. We'd watch her putting her bike up against the shop window. As soon as she was in the shop we'd strike. One method was to take off the oily chain, and of course be ready to offer to put it back on when the mot came out of the shop. Our dirty, oily hands, having rubbed them well on the bike chain, never failed to impress the mots of our gentle manners. Another method was to let the air out of one of the tubes and pretend she had a puncture. While the mot was biting her lip and wondering what she'd do we were all action. 'Get the loan of two forks and a basin of water, missus, would you have a loan of two forks and a basin of water, has anyone got a repair kit?' And somebody always had a repair kit and some oul' wan always had a basin and two forks. The mot and the mot's pals would be chatted up to the eyeballs while the job would be in progress. 'You're a nice fella,' the mot would say. God if they only knew they'd have wrapped the bikes around our necks. But in a way we were young gentlemen. We always stood up in a tram or a bus to let a girl or a lady sit down.

Hikes, picnics and bike tours all started on St. Patrick's Day. Hail, rain or snow, St. Patrick's Day will turn the stone and let the sun shine! Sitting in the Pine Forest like drowned rats eating the mot's banana sandwiches and fairy cakes and hiding our thick cuts of bread and jam. In our early teens it was the age of 'the party'. At the drop of a hat someone would have a party. There were only millions of parties. And they always seemed to be in a house with a piano, or Joe Hanna as we called them. The party would start at ten o'clock at night and end up at six o'clock Mass on Sunday morning and home to bed. (After a while I got browned off with parties as they always ruined the Sunday which was always the best day of the week.) To the party you had to bring a present. I don't know what we would have done only for Hector Grey. At that time Hector had a small office in Abbey Street and he sold massive jewellery at tenpence. I remember buying a lovely brooch in a lovely box for ten-pence. That night at the party the girl got ten of the same brooch.

I was at a posh party one time. How I know it was a posh party was that they had a twenty-two piece tea-set. The extra piece was a slop bowl, a little bowl the same size as the sugar bowl for throwing your tea leaves into after your first cup of tea. At all the other parties the second cup of tea went in on the remains of the first cup, but at the posh party the remains of the first cup went into the slop bowl. It was the first and last slop bowl I've seen to this day. I'll never forget that slop bowl. It was a sit-down-at-the-table affair, not like the cup-and-saucer-and-plate-on-your-knee affair, and me trying to do a juggle act with six others sitting on the sofa. No, this mot was class and so was her mother and so was the slop bowl, until I made a mistake and threw me tea leaves into the sugar bowl. Now if the makers of china tea-sets ever intend to bring back the slop bowl, for God's sake and for my sake will yis paint it a different colour.

The piano, the sing song, the crowded dancing, the lights out when the mother was in the kitchen, postman's knock, spin the bottle, forfeits and kisses by the dozen!

Clicking the mots led to dates and blind dates. A blind date for the Metropole foyer. I went on a few blind dates and I even went along with one fella who was too shy to go out with the girl on her own. There was the three of us sitting in the gods of the Rialto cinema, he on one side, me on the other and the mot in the middle. The next day he told me that he thought the mot was very mean. 'How's that?' I asked. 'Well,' said he, 'I gave her a small box of chocolates in the picture house and then I held her hand but she never offered the chocolates all night.' What he didn't know was that I was holding her right hand and unless she could open a box of chocolates with her feet there was no hope of your man getting a sweet.

The dates, the Metropole foyer with everyone looking at everyone else, the comings and goings, the clock watching, the stand ups, the late late comers, the glamour, the excitement, and the usher telling the two queues that the big picture was ten minutes started. I remember one date I had for the Metropole foyer. I had five shillings in my pocket. We had two plain teas in the Capitol restaurant for one shilling and eight pence. Do you remember the Capitol with the little red romantic lamps on each table? Pot of tea, brown bread, white bread, scones and jam. Two shilling tickets in the Metropole cinema, a quarter of chocolate sweets for a shilling. I still had fourpence for the bus fare home out of five bob. If you were in the money you could have rasher, egg, sausage, tea and bread and butter for three shillings and sixpence.

The dance was the 'hop'. 'Will ye buy a ticket for a hop in the Slipper. They're only a shilling and there's a spot-prize for every waltz.' And how we hopped at all the hophalls in danceland Dublin. The butchers, the bakers, the bricklayers, the teachers. At the Swiss Chalet, the Adelaide, the CYMS, the Classic in Duke Street which was a skating rink as well, the Orpheus in South Anne Street with its maple floor and whose owners never allowed the dancehall to be overcrowded as we hopped around like sardines. The local hop was Arus Mhuire with memories of Father Devine making sure no mot was sitting on your knee.

Parnell Square was the capital of danceland. The Galway Arms where you couldn't swing a cat, it was like a tu'penny stamp, but many's a good hop we had in it. The A.O.H. had the wall mirrors to let you see yourself hopping, and with Brian Boru, the High King of Ireland, looking at you doing a military two-step to the music of Charlie Shaw's band. There was the Rose Bowl, Roseland, Banba, Balilika, Ierne and the Hotel St. George which as known far and wide as Conarchys. Believe it or believe it not, I was a member of the Kerryman's Association that got in for half price to all the Kerrymen's dances in Conarchys. I worked with a Kerryman and he gave me the first free brief for their Friday night dance. Every dance a spot, take ten paces down the hall, stop, turn right, take two paces, stop, turn left, the couple in front of you a spot-prize — two free briefs for a dance in the Castle Ballroom, music by Bobby Murphy with Bridie Howitt. Next spot-prize, ten Players Please cigarettes for the gent, box of chocolates for the lady. The box of chocolates was about the same size as the ten Players with about eight sweets in it. Free cycle parks, ladies half-hour, one and sixpence before nine. The Paley Glide, the Rotunda Winter Garden, the Ballerina, the Town and Country Club, the Cuckoo's Nest, Romanoffs, call it what you may but it's the same halls and walls have witnessed some hops and sweats down the years from yer granny's day. I think a word of thanks is due to Mr. Morosini Whelan, Mr. James Butler and Miss Bercha Dixon who taught us how to do the quickstep, foxtrot, samba and tango and gave us demonstrations of ballroom dancing that would make Fred Astaire and Ginger Rogers blush.

Out of town dancing was by bus from Aston's Quay to the Eagle's Nest, Bray, and back again for four shillings. If we didn't pick up a mot on the way down, or if we didn't pick up a mot at the dance, we never failed to pick up a mot on the bus home.

We didn't follow any particular dance band but we knew them all from Johnny Devlin and Johnny Butler to Jim Bacon, Johnny Keyes and a host of others.

The dancing night of the year was the dress dance. Dress dance at the Gresham Hotel, music by Jimmy Masson and the resident orchestra, dancing 9–3, supper at 10 p.m. At the Metropole it was music by Phil Murtagh. What a thrill every dress dance was! Picking your mot, asking her, organising the hire of the dress suit. Down to Nearys, Capel Street, to check the price. Then down to Smiths, Hawkins Street, for another quote. Someone always said that yer man on the quays was cheaper. What man, what quays? Above Capel Street Bridge, up and down stairways. Mister, di ya hire out dress suits? On a wet night yer man on the quays gave goloshes to protect the dancing shoes. The dress suit, tails, dickie bow, white shirt – dancing shoes with no heels on them cost three shillings extra. Deposit paid, hire charges paid. The suit and shoes were always packed in a big brown cardboard box with a warning written on it in red ink: 'Must be returned before 3 p.m. the following day or deposit forfeited.' As I walked up the quays with the box everyone knew I'd hired a dress suit. You could see all the smiles on the people's faces then. Some hardchaw would roar out across the street, 'Hey you, come back with the dress suit. Are you going to a hop in the Gresham. Where's the dress dance, Mack?' It was no different on the bus. Everyone was talking about dress dances, and the woman beside me kept reading out loud the warning about 3 p.m. and the deposit. Home at last, the wash up, the shave, the dressing up in the dress suit. 'You're lovely, but the tails is a bit long, could you not have got a smaller tails?' Instead of being twelve foot tall I was now only two foot over a jam jar as I made me way to the mot's house. The mots were never ready, and oh God the waiting, with the mot's mother giving the dress suit the once over forty times. 'The tails are a bit long.' Then the terrible bus journey with everyone on the bus asking could I not afford a taxi. The tickets, the box of chocolates for the mot and the photograph money would leave me broke for a month and yer man wanting me to take a taxi as well. 'She's lucky she's not on the crossbar of my bike.' I did bring one mot on me bike. Can you imagine me in me dress suit and tails, dancing shoes and goloshes, and the mot on the crossbar with her long (hired) dress up around her ears to prevent it catching in the spokes.

The hum of excitement in the Gresham, the music, the coloured lights, balloons, streamers, paper hats, gold crowns, Paul Jones and the mot glittering like a film star. Supper at 10 p.m. Who cares if the soup goes cold? Non-stop dancing. Who cares what the photos are like? Who cares if the tails are too long? I'm in Heaven and Fred Astaire is only in the ha'penny place.

3

Lent in Ould God's Time

EVERY 'HANSEL MONDAY' I got a new pair of short trousers with 'Hansel money' in the pockets. A ha'penny, or a penny, or if times were good, a silver thru'penny bit, with a rabbit on one side and a harp on the other. Every Shrove Tuesday we got pancakes by the dozen; sometimes we even had a lemon to squeeze on the pancakes. But the old dip in the sugar bowl (when the mother wasn't looking) was a flavour hard to beat. Every Ash Wednesday we got Holy Ashes. 'Remember man, thou art but dust and into dust thou shalt return'.

Some priests were real dingers at giving out the ashes. Dead straight, right in the centre, a real professional job. Other priests, God bless them, were bad shots with their thumbs. Oh! many's the time the ashes ended up in me hair and other times they nearly ended up in me eye. Another thing was the quality and the colour of the ashes. Now, we liked the black-as-soot ashes, which gave us something to show for our Faith. We had no time for the light brown coloured ashes, that sprinkled down our noses. Sure a fella could get that type of ash in the fire grate any day of the week. Outside the church, the gang were waiting to give the result; 'He missed you, go back for another'.

But ashes was a bit like Holy Communion, once you had it, you had it, no going back for another. So a fella was lucky to get a good black spot right in the centre of the forehead.

Ashes to Ashes,
Dust to Dust,
If God won't have you,
The Devil must.

Then we all charged home to look in the mirror and give the result to ourselves. The priest made the sign of the cross putting on the ashes but all we were left with was the priest's thumb print. Anyone who had anything that even looked like a cross, well that was a miracle, or yer man was a saint. Sometimes, while washing our faces, we washed off the ashes by mistake. Now, we knew how Adam and Eve felt leaving the Garden of Eden Ash Wednesday and no ashes to show. 'Hey, did yeh not get your ashes?' or 'Are you a Proddy?'

> Proddy, Proddy on the wall,
> Half a loaf to feed yis all,
> A farthing candle to show yis light,
> To read the Bible on a Saturday night.

Well, many's the Saturday night I had me farthing candle, only God forgive me, I wasn't reading the Bible. No, it was all them penny horribles, ·*The Dandy, The Beano, The Hotspur, The Wizard,* and *The Rover.* 'Any swops, Mac?'

The next thing after the ashes was 'the giving up'. Someone's old fella was giving up the 'drink' and the 'smokes' for Lent. How can you follow that? The 'giving up' took over everything, from sweets, pictures, dances, fruit, bikes, trams, hikes, football and courting. Everyone was giving up something for Lent. Indeed, the sanctity on the street corner would make the Saints blush. Everyone was out doing everyone else, 'giving up' became the fashion. After the ashes and the 'giving up' the next thing was the Lenten Fast. One main meal and two small collations. Dry bread, black tea, meat only once a day, no meat on Wednesday or Friday. All Fridays were Fast days, and the other days were days of abstinence. It's funny how you get hungry when you know you can't have it. Well, we fasted and fasted and fasted. Then one Sunday at Mass, the priest said that people were not to worry too much about the fast. Now, for the two collations, he said, 'You can have a little fish, an egg or a little cheese.' I felt like saying, 'Father, if we had a little fish, we'd have it for the main meal.' We thought cheese was the thing you said, when you were getting your photograph taken. 'Unless you do penance, you shall all likewise perish.' Even a kid with a cut of bread and jam was frowned on.

> Out of hell, there's no redemption,
> There you get your weekly pension,
> Fourpence a week for working hard
> Chasing the Devil around the yard.

And to chase the Devil out of the parish the Missioners were coming. The first week for women, the second week for men, and the boys and girls in between. The Missioners were the order priests. There was always a big Missioner and a little Missioner, or a fat Missioner and a skinny Missioner, or a funny Missioner and a Missioner that no one liked. I often remember being glued to the seat in the chapel, half afraid to go home in case Old Nick, the Devil himself, was outside waiting to grab me. It was always the funny fella who roared like a bull and made the hairs stand out on the back of my neck. the final night of the Mission we all bought a candle for a shilling to renounce the world, the flesh and the Devil. Old Nick got it that night.

> Some say the Devil is dead,
> Some say he's hardy,
> Some say he's down in hell
> Eating sugar barley.
> Some say the Devil is dead,
> Some say he's hardy,
> Some say he's gone away
> To join the British Army.

Then, we discovered that we could buy second-hand candles for fourpence and save eightpence. 'Candles only fourpence each here.' These candles were the ones the women used at their Mission and were only burned down about an inch. So we started buying the second-hand candles until one of the gang produced a brand new candle in the middle of all the second-hand ones; we got such a fright that we nearly forgot to give Old Nick the works. After the Mission, the fella with the new candle said that he was afraid that our candles, the second-hand ones, had no effect on yer man, Old Nick himself. From that day on we all bought new candles for a shilling, and did without the twenty Woodbines we got for the eightpence.

The only mid-Lent break was St. Patrick's Day. Good old St. Patrick, he started the hiking season, turned the stone and changed the weather. He'd have some job nowadays. On St. Patrick's Day we could eat sweets and if we had the Guino (money) we could have the pics. The only other break in Lent was the Passion Play in the Oblate Fathers' Hall. The rumour went all around Inchicore that Father Allen was playing the part of Our Lord Jesus Christ. With Father Allen in the lead role we were all looking forward to the Passion Play. He was our sodality priest, and we all loved him. Well, imagine our disappointment when some fella out of Inchicore, one of the Amps Players, was in the lead role and no sign of Father Allen, and to make matters worse we were all thrown out for booing Judas.

It was the only time the Bishop wrote to us. His letter was so long that they could only read a bit of it each Sunday. The Bishop said all sorts of things that we didn't understand. We all knew that we couldn't go to school in Trinity College. Poor Dubliners banned from Trinity by mortal sins and money. The long gospel at Mass was the long gospel, not like today, reading only what is underlined. There were no lines in God's ould time. Mass was every half hour on a Sunday, sometimes we had to fight our way into the church with the crowds coming out. Then the clergy decided to have Mass every hour to ease the crowd situation, but the sermons got longer and we still had the weekly fights. Up in Rathmines Chapel there was a character named 'Ashes and Sackcloth'. He stood at the chapel door watching the girls going into the chapel with short skirts and low-cut blouses. 'Ah Ah,' he'd say, pointing to the skirt and blouse, 'Ashes and sackcloth for you, me miss, ashes and sackcloth.' The poor girls ran into the chapel with one hand pulling down the skirt and the other hand pulling up the blouse. Holy Thursday was the day for visiting the seven chapels. On Good Friday we all went to kiss the cross and to do the Stations of the Cross, then it was home like hell for the hot cross buns.

On Easter Saturday we all went to the pics to see if Flash Gordon was still alive. After the pics we'd be brought up to date on Flash Gordon and the 'follyinupper' by some pagan, who had given nothing up for Lent. Easter Sunday and Easter eggs. The eggs were always in an egg cup or a mug and an extra treat was a few of Woolworth's marshmallows. We always wore the green, white and orange Easter Lily in memory of Easter Week 1916. In the evening time we were brought to Arbour Hill, to the graves of Pearse, Connolly and the other leaders of the Rising.

> Green, White and Yellow,
> Me Mother had a fellow,
> The fella died,
> Me Mother cried,
> Green, White and Yellow.

4

Starve the Barber

WHAT ARE WE GOING to do today for a chase and a bit of gas? I'm fed up rattling ashbins, knocking on doors, singing outside barber shops and shouting after men on bikes, 'Hey you, your back wheel is catching up on the front one. Get down and milk it . . . Where are yeh going with no bell on yer bike. Come back if you like.' And if yer man made the slightest sign of coming back, we ran like hell. Oh many's the good chase I got all around Inchicore and Kilmainham and up and down the lanes of the South Circular Road at the back of the swanky houses. The maze of lanes were a great getaway on a chase, until the day I ran up the dead-end lane and was cornered up against the high wall. The barber in his white coat with the black razor strap swinging was coming in closer and closer. 'I'll Billy the Barber yeh,' he shouted, 'I'll cut yer bloody head off,' as he fingered the two razors sticking out. of his top pocket. 'Oh mister, mister, I'm sorry, I won't do it again, mister, honest I won't.' I waited my chance until he was nearly on top of me. He was breathless, panting hard, his face as red as a turkey cock. 'I'll,' pant, 'Billy,' pant, 'the,' pant, 'Barber,' and just at that moment I went out under his arms and swinging strap like the greyhound Mick the Miller leaving his box in Shelbourne Park. I didn't look back to see if the barber was coming nor did I stop until I was safe in the new park at Islandbridge which had no dead-end lanes, only wide open spaces and even the Liffey to swim across if it

32

Billy the Barber,
Shaved his father,
With the rusty razor,
The razor slipped,
And cut his lip,
Hurrah for Billy the Barber.

came to that. Later that evening I was still picking the small beard hairs off me red gansey. You see, not only did I get a chase that day, I got a belt of the wooden mug which was half full of dirty, soapy, hairy water as well. As soon as we started our singing, the barber's door opened and out came the shaving mug. Nine out of ten times it missed me. But on the tenth time it splattered all over me red gansey. I don't think I ever got all those little beard hairs out of me gansey even after me mother boiled it and rubbed it on the wooden washing board with carbolic soap. I think that was the last time I sang outside the barber shops.

Hair and barber shops played a very important part in our growing up. The mother was always watching me hair and every Saturday night was spent listening to the balladmakers on the wireless and searching for nits with the little white fine comb. The terror of our childhood was ringworm, but thank God I never got that. The mother always decided when it was time to get a haircut, 'I think yeh need a haircut. How much does yer man in Old Kilmainham charge?' 'Thru'pence, ma, but he gaps ya. It's fourpence in Martins and it's the same price where Mikey Kavanagh works.' 'Right, here's fourpence, go to Mikey Kavanagh and tell him I want a nice short back and sides.' The mother needn't have been watching my hair at all. Sure all Inchicore and Kilmainham was watching it for her. As soon as me hair got long I couldn't walk ten yards without someone shouting, 'Hey, hey you with the head, don't walk under a barber's pole, it might fall on ya . . . Hey you, starve the barber.' Then when I got me hair cut every kid I met wet the top of his fingers with his tongue and slapped his wet fingers on me new haircut and said, 'Hansel. Janey Mack he scalped you, but don't worry, the hair restorer hair oil will grow it quick again.' We were convinced that the barber's homemade hair oil was really hair restorer to get you back again for another haircut.

'Me Mammy said I don't want any hair oil.'

'Ah, I'll just put on a drop, tell your mother you have a dry scalp.'

There was always a message from me ma to the barber and

a message from the barber back to me ma. 'Tell your mother I had to comb it that way. You have a calf's lick.' Everything was licks. A calf's lick when me hair wouldn't go right. A hand lick for to hansel new haircuts. A cat's lick when I went for the bread. A lick of your Johnny Ray's wafer outside the Tivo in Francis Street. And the threat of having the daylights licked out of me if I didn't come in before night to do me ecker.

Do you know what, the Beatles have a lot to answer for. They're the fellas that brought in the long hair that nearly starved the barbers. And then the people shifting the blame off the Beatles on to the Sacred Heart. The writing was on the wall for many barber shops when the clergy and Christian Brothers started wearing long hair. When I was a child the only people in Dublin who wore long hair were the poets in Trinity, Hairy Lemon, Hairy Yank and Johnny Forty Coats. The yanks too must take some of the blame with their crew cut styles. And that other fella, 'Teddy Boy', who brought in the D.A. style — the duck's arse. We must have been all losing our marbles. We really weren't the full shilling looking for a duck's arse for the back of our necks. There was a time when we didn't even want a red neck like a country man, and then suddenly we were all going round like the ducks in Stephen's Green. Do you know what, I think the poets in Trinity College should all go back to the short back and sides styles and show up all the hairy fellows.

Hair is now really gone to hell. Ya have fellas now growing their locks right down to their chins, half-moon beards, and where is the lovely Errol Flynn and Don Ameche ronnie of yesterday? Where in Dublin can you see a waxed moustache pointed like a darning needle instead of those that look like the walrus out of the azoo? The poor ladies are no different. In my day it was a club perm for a wave or a bob. Now it's the Shaggy, the Afro, the Purdy, the Punk, the Page Boy, the Urchin, His and Hers, unisex, hair transplants, Renato of Rome, Witches Hut, hairstudios! I went into a His and Hers lately and had me hair attended to by a lady. It was the first time a lady attended me hair since me mother searched for nits on a Saturday night with the fine comb. 'We have to wash it first, mister,' the lady said. So me hair was washed and half dried and then it was cut by another lady. She seemed to be doing a good job, so I decided to get me beard trimmed. I asked her, 'Will you trim my beard please?' 'Oh Janey,' said she, 'I never trimmed a beard, mister. I don't think I could trim a beard. Janey, no, mister.' 'That's all right,' I said, 'I get it done elsewhere.' I looked in the mirror and saw that she was worried. Before I could say anything she roared down the shop, 'Lucy, Lucy, do you know anything about trimming beards?' Lucy roared back, 'No, Jacintha, I don't know anything about trimming beards.' There was a slight pause of silence in the shop, then Lucy roared back, 'I don't know anything about beards, Jacintha, but I suppose it's the same as cutting heads only it's upside down.'

I'd nearly go as far as to say that An Taisce should have taken over all the old barber shops and preserved them for posterity. I learned more about life in the barber shops of Dublin than any college student did in his university. The barber shop was unique. Some barbers had their red and white pole standing up straight like a soldier while others had theirs sticking out the window like a flagpole. But sure they didn't need the pole as a sign. Everyone knew their own favourite barber shop. It was like a day's outing on a Saturday sitting in the barber shop waiting on your turn, who was before you and who was after yeh, the place a hive of chatter, the passing and swopping of *Picture Post* magazines, reading all the barber's signs and watching the cut hair form little mountains on the floor. Now and again as the hair mountain grew, the barber left the customer, picked up the sweeping brush, swept the hair and placed it in a potato sack. I often saw two sacks full of hair in Johnny's shop on Emmet Road. That was the hair that would be sent to the factory to make wigs for baldy men, or so we believed. In Weaver Square the wall sign read, 'Irish Curled Hair Manufacturer'. And there were several hair-dyeing and wig-making factories in Dublin. Even the baldy man didn't escape the jeering. He may not have been a starve the barber, but to one and all he was baldy conscience, and we didn't begrude him our spare hair to make a wig.

The hairs didn't only fall on the floor. They fell everywhere. Down the back of the neck, on the nose, and all over the white sheet that covered me chest and knees. One barber who was fond of a drop used to blow the hairs off me nose with his mouth and the smell of porter would nearly have me drunk. Each barber had his own style of cutting, standing and talking. Some stood like ballet dancers on one toe, others with feet well apart and yet others with their knees dug into your chest like a dentist. They all talked to me face in the mirror and the scissors never stopped clipping, even when it was a foot over me head. The barber not only shaved faces and cut hair but he was an authority on football, horse racing, greyhounds, doubles, trebles and coupons and advice on any matter. I heard the barber say, 'Hollow ground razors should be sharpened on the palm of the hand and let the natural oil of the skin do the sharpening. Never mind them oil stones and leather straps. The palm of the hand. But be careful with the fingers.' The ash from the Woodbine cigarette never fell as the smoke blinded the barber's eye, but still he clipped, clipped, clipped at the small hairs around me ears, and I watching carefully in the mirror and praying for me ear. The only time the barber left me was to turn and twist the knobs in his Cosser wireless which gave forth a cracking noise and an Oxford accent giving the racing results at 6 p.m.

I'll never forget the first time the electric clippers came to Inchicore. It doesn't hurt, it doesn't pinch, it tiddles yeh. So we all went for a tiddle instead of a pinch. One barber who stuck to the old hand clippers used to say that a man in Carlow was electrocuted by an electric hair clipper. 'After all,' he'd say, 'I might take a lump out of your neck but at least you're still alive.' 'Free haircuts tomorrow . . . Why go to the dogs anywhere else, all the best hairs are here . . . Remember, we need your head to run our business.'

When we became teenagers we used to go into town on a

Saturday and now and again we'd go to a fancy barber shop in O'Connell Street or Westmoreland Street. They were called hairdressing salons and they used to put cotton wool on the back of the neck to prevent the hairs going down the collar. As the haircutting ended, you were asked if you would like dressing and were given the choice of several hair oils, creams and brilliantine liquid or solid and a neck spray with talcum powder. After the barbers we used to stand on O'Connell Bridge and say, 'There it is, there it is.' Before long half of O'Connell Street would be looking up into the air at nothing. Whenever we played that game as children we always added the following street rhyme:

> We made ya look,
> We made ya stare,
> We made the barber
> Cut your hair.
> He cut it long,
> He cut it short,
> He cut it with a knife and fork.

Now everyone knows that the only kitchen utensil used for cutting hair is the pudding bowl. Not everyone went to the barber on a Saturday for a haircut. No, some kids got homemade or do-it-yourself haircuts from their ma or da. In such cases the pudding bowl was put on the child's head and all the hair under the rim of the bowl was cut. They were bang on free haircuts. The only trouble was that the child's head looked like a pudding bowl. 'Hey you, did yer mother cut your hair with the pudding bowl?' Other free haircuts were given at the technical school — models for students they called it. It was worse than the dental in Lincoln Place. At least no one could see the bad workmanship inside your mouth, but Janey Mack the gaps and gashes in the free technical school haircuts had us all looking like Mohawk Indians.

How many remember the demon barber in Capel Street? He used to pawn his five razors every Monday and redeem them every Friday. Coming down Capel Street from the pawn shop he'd offer cut-price shaves. Wet or dry he'd shave his customers in Capel Street using the waterpipe in the yard of the old tenement houses.

To all barbers, hairdressers, stylists, His and Hers of today and yesterday, I take off me hat to yis and that's a compliment because I can get a haircut now with me hat on. The only time I ever feel like a millionaire is after a haircut when the barber is brushing down me ol' suit.

5

Paddy on the Railway

THE GREAT SOUTHERN and Western Railway played a major part in our street education. It taught us how to make screwdrivers, put ball racers on a gig or boxcar and make the price of the pics. As the passengers got off the train at Kingsbridge (Sean Heuston) lugging their suitcases, we were ready to offer our services. 'Missus, will I carry your case? ' Carrying cases was tough work. I think some ould wans had cases full of turnips, the weight of some of them would pull the arm out of your sockets at the shoulder. Nevertheless we lugged them, dragged them, and pushed them all over the Parkgate and James's Street. Sometimes it was for tu'pence, sometimes it was for a penny, and sometimes they only said 'Thank you'. I think half of the ould wans thought we were going to run away with their cases, some chance we'd have, Samson would not be able to run with some of the cases I've carried. On a good day we'd make the price of the pics and have one arm longer than the other.

Screwdrivers were made by putting six inch nails on the rail tracks. The old iron horse steam engines, which we called 'Puff Puffs', then turned the nails into screwdrivers. We had screwdrivers by the dozen and spent manys the day looking for customers. 'Mister will yeh buy a few screwdrivers, they're only six a penny.' Screwdrivers must have been very cheap, because I don't think we ever sold any.

The ball racers were magic. Anyone with a gig with ball

Paddy on the Railway,
Picking up Stones,
Up comes the Engine and chops
Off his nose.
Oh, says Paddy, that's not fair.
Oh, says the engine, I don't care!

racers would be elected head of the gang without any opposition. Broken ball racers provided the big steelers for playing marbles. One big steeler was worth one hundred glassers and a thousand white chalkers. For 'Taw in the Hole' or 'Up along the Gully' the steeler was in a class of his own. The railway works at Inchicore provided all the six inch nails and ball racers. 'Mister, any nails, Mister, any ball racers? ' Some days we were lucky, and some days we didn't get a light. 'Go up to the Spa Road Works,' said one workman. 'They have plenty of ball racers.' The Spa Road Works was where they made the trams. So we all charged down past the Dining Hall and Dan Wall's Billiard Saloon, around by the Black Lion, Lavins, and Edwards Cake Shop and up the Spa Road. 'Mister, any nails, any ball racers? No, son, sorry, try Toffs.'

Do hobby horses have ball racers? Toffs were hobby horse makers. Well, we didn't get any nails or ball racers but we got plenty of goes on the hobby horses until the yard man told us to try Brassingtons. Ah, let's go and look at the Grotto Boy. We'd cross the road and enter the Oblate Fathers' grounds, pay a quick visit to the church and the grotto and sneak down by the Retreat House and climb up on a certain window sill and gaze in wonder at the Grotto Boy. He was lying in a glass coffin and we could see the blood on his neck where his father had cut his throat with an open razor. The Grotto Boy never failed to thrill us, I've heard at least six different stories as to how he died. The most popular story was that the boy's father didn't believe in God and forbade his son to go to Mass. One Sunday morning the father was asleep, so the boy crept out of bed and went to seven o'clock Mass in the Oblate Church. After Mass, the father was waiting at the church gate, his face half shaved and he had the razor in his hand. When the son would not agree to stay away from Mass, the father killed him. 'Right where you're standing'. We used to look down at the ground at the gate to see if any of the boy's blood was still to be seen. Any black marks on the ground were taken as bloodstains. Clinging on the narrow window sill, eyes full of wonder, mind full of mystery, and your ears full of 'hurry up and give us a decko at the Grotto Boy'.

Carrying cases, making screwdrivers, putting ball racers on a gig, steelers, puff puffs, Grotto Boy and the Oblate Fathers' Church, none of it would have been possible without the Great Southern and Western, and Paddy on the Railway and his fellow Railway workers. Let's give three cheers for them all. So here's to the first railway men who put ball racers on a gig and introduced steelers into the game of marbles. And here's to the first railmen who cut the first sods and laid the first rails of the Great Southern and Western Railway. Here's to the railway workers who built the Oblate Fathers' Church in Inchicore in thirteen hours.

Kingsbridge terminus was chosen for many reasons. It was near the Cattle, Fruit, Hay and Vegetable Markets. It was near the Liffey to tie up with shipping, it was midway between north and south Dublin. It was near the Vice-Regal Lodge in the Park, but most important of all it was a vital link up with the British Military Command at the Curragh Camp and it was near enough to the Royal and Richmond Barracks, Parkgate and Dublin Castle.

In January 1845 a descendant of Lord Edward Fitzgerald's family cut the first sod near Adamstown Castle. The Duke of Leinster took off his coat, rolled up his sleeves, and with the skill of a good able workman, cut the first six sods. He then lifted them onto the shovel, put them into a wheel barrow and dumped them at the side of the field, while the band played, the bunting waves, and the people cheered. By August 1846 the first trial trips were under way from Dublin to Carlow. The building at Kingsbridge was designed by Santon Woods and it is one of the most beautiful buildings in the city. Floodlit at night time it stands like a massive stone king, looking down on Anna Livia's reflecting waters. The railway works and the railway workers' houses at Inchicore is nearly another city in itself with four separate towns. The town of Ring Street, where Peadar Kearney, the author of our national anthem, the 'Tri-Coloured Ribbon', and many other national ballads, lived and died. The Bungalow, as some people called it, was named after the famous Father Ring. It would take a book to tell the story of how the Protestant Boy from Portstewart in the County of Derry became an Oblate Priest and was the first man to lead the Oblate Pilgrimage to Lourdes. The town of Inchicore north was called 'The Ranch'. An old man told me that *his* grandfather told him that when he was a child, Inchicore north was all fields except for the railway houses, three country mansions and a public house. The town of Inchicore south with its old tavern, the Black Lion, the meeting place for Fenians and the Invincibles, the rally point for monster election meetings, the crossing point for the ancient Camac River, Grattan Crescent and the gateway to South Terrace and the lovable Dining Hall for hops, hooleys and fancy dress parties. What kid in Inchicore didn't win a two pound pot of Scott's Strawberry Jam or a box of Fry's Shell Cocoa or a voucher for Stumps or Roger's Pork Shops?

In the town of Goldenbridge was the site of the old Spa, where Dubliners came to drink and bathe in its holy healing waters. The Tram Sheds, Toffs, the Sisters of Mercy and the 'Puck'. 'Do you know why they call it the Puck? ' said the man in the doorway in Thomas Davis Street. 'Well I'll tell you,' he said. Jem Larkin loved this spot and when the food pucks came up the Liffey in 1913, during the lock-out, Larkin ordered a few pucks to be sent to Goldenbridge. This is the very spot where they shared out the pucks, ever since it's known as the 'Puck'.

Father Mulcahy, a curate in St. Audoen's, High Street, used to walk daily to Inchicore, saying his Office. One day he was resting on Inchicore Hill and a few railway men passed by. They saluted each other, then one of the railway men said, 'Hey, Father, when are yis going to build a church in Inchore? ' The priest laughed and said as soon as he became a bishop. But, before the priest left the hill, he took a Miraculous Medal from his pocket, dug a small hole with his boot and buried the medal. 'Now, Mary, Mother of God, it's up to you to get your church built here for the people of Inchicore.' A short time later Father Mulcahy took ill and was confined to bed with a bad fever, and for several weeks it was touch and go. Then the fever left him and he made a quick recovery. A nurse told him about the new church in Inchicore. He took a cab to Inchicore Hill and saw the new wooden church right on the spot where he had buried the Miraculous Medal. After praying in thanksgiving at the high altar, he went in search of someone to tell him how the church came to be built on this very spot.

It seemed that in the year 1856 Fathers Fox, Gubbins, Cooke and Arnoux, members of the Oblates of Mary Immaculate came to the Augustinians in John's Lane to give a Mission. As the Mission closed, Fathers Fox, Gubbins and Arnoux returned to Yorkshire. But Father Cooke remained on a few days in Dublin to rest. He then visited the Archbishop to get permission to set up a house in Dublin. 'Where do you intend to set up a house?' said the Archbishop. Father Cooke was taken by surprise and found the word Kilmainham on his lips. 'Good,' said the Archbishop, 'That's the only suburb in Dublin that is not covered by a religious body, go ahead and set up your house.'

Father Cooke and a few friends from John's Lane did a tour of the lands of Kilmainham and in the end bought the land on Inchicore Hill. They said Mass in a private house nearby and after Mass Father Cooke told the people that they needed a new church but where would they get one? A young railway carpenter spoke up. 'Father, if you get the timber, glass and nails, I'll undertake to build a wooden church to hold a thousand people, in a week!' It was such an impossible undertaking that the priest said, 'Why not make it two thousand people?' 'Right,' said yer man, 'leave it to me and you'll see.'

The next day, Tuesday 24th June 1856, the materials were ordered and delivered to the site. At six o'clock that evening, seven hundred men and the young carpenter arrived on the site, with their hammers, saws, shovels, spades, barrows and picks. Each evening, after a hard day's work, the men came, until the last nail was driven home on Saturday night at ten o'clock. In thirteen hours the railway men of Inchicore had built a chapel, had made an altar and had made seating for over a thousand people. The railway men did more; they later built a grotto, similar to Lourdes, and many of them gave their sons to the Congregation of Mary Immaculate.

Like as I was saying, 'Paddy on the Railway' did a little more than picking up stones!

6

Damn the Weather

MARY DOYLE, whoever she was, was fond of hairy old fellas. The only man I ever saw with a marble eye was old 'one eye ball' himself. He was a devil for plucking out the eye and offering it to chisellers on the palm of his dirty hand. Some said it was only a joke because we never saw the empty eye socket. He kept that closed tight while he rolled the marble eye around his hand.

'Feel it,' he'd say, but we ran like hell. Then he'd shout after us, 'Come back yes blackguards and feel me marble eye.' We wouldn't go back for a thousand pounds. Whenever I see the sign of an eye over an optician's shop I always think of old one eye ball. His favourite haunt was around the back of the pipes and Cork Street. Sometimes he'd catch us in the narrow lane at the back of the pipes and spread out his arms to prevent us passing. 'Wait now,' he'd say, 'till I show yis the marble eye.' He made a sound with his mouth as he plucked it out. The effect on us was worse than the Banshee or the Green Lady who walked on the green canal waters after dark, but this was broad daylight and our hair was standing up straight. We were all great runners, but somehow the plucking of the eye took our breaths away and before we got to James's Walk or Maryland we were panting.

In a way old one eye ball looked like Damn the Weather. He had the same type of hairy face and they both wore long black coats turned grey from wear and age, and both wore no

The rain, the rain,
The rain blew high,
The rain came falling from the sky.
Mary Doyle said she'd die
If she didn't get the fella
With the marble eye.

The Use of an
Umbrella.

hats and open neck shirts. Damn the Weather was my favourite character in Dublin.

> Summer's too bloody hot,
> Winter's too bloody cold,
> Spring is only for lambs
> and Autumn for cleaning trees.
> Oh, oh, oh, damn the weather.

In summer or winter Damn the Weather wore the same old clothes. I think he damned the summer more than he damned the winter. Thomas Street and the Liberties was his favourite haunt and he used to dine with all his fellow characters in John's Lane Church beside the hot pipes. The hot wall in Bridgefoot Street, where Thompson's Bakery ovens baked the bread on one side and heat the poor of Dublin on the other side was only used in the mornings and early afternoons. A regular line up at the hot wall included Johnny Forty Coats, Damn the Weather, Hairy Yank, Hairy Lemon, Shell Shock Joe, and the Bugler Dunne. Bang Bang didn't seem to mind the weather as he raced from tram to tram shooting half of Dublin with his '45 door key.

The lady characters seldom used the hot wall. All Parcels was busy collecting waste paper and tieing it into little parcels, while Nancy Needleballs seemed to spend her whole day sitting on the footpath in High Street.

The Stephen's Green — Merrion Square wards of Dublin are alive with lady and gent characters today. The Circle Woman, who looks like an American university graduate and spends her days walking around in circles in Stephen's Green, The Blue Lady with prayers and holy pictures seems to favour the gates of Leinster House. The gent with flowing beard and gown and the bough of a tree favours Baggot Street and Blackrock. The difference between today's street characters and the street characters of my childhood is that they seem better dressed, better fed and better educated.

But then old Hairy Yank was supposed to have been a millionaire who lost all his money in the Wall Street crash of 1929. While others were throwing themselves off the Empire State Building old Hairy Yank returned to Dublin to sell cabbage plants — one hundred cabbage plants, planted and all for one shilling and threepence. He'd chat up the lady of the house first, 'Oh but you're a lovely looking woman, you should have been a film star. How about a nice few cabbage plants in the garden?' Rudolf Valentino couldn't have done better. Among all the giggles and blushes the cabbage plants were sold and planted. That night, after dark, Hairy Yank came back, pulled up all the cabbage plants and the next day sold them to the woman next door. The cabbage plants went down along the avenue like Darkie Bluebells.

Johnny Forty Coats was also from well off stock. His name was Jack Russell, his father was a doctor, he was an only child and his father died when he was sixteen years of age. The story among the old dealers around Thomas Street is that after the father's death the mother took up with another man. Jack got jealous and told the mother that if she intended to marry her fancy man he was moving out. The mother got married and Jack hit the streets.

This Johnny Forty Coats, the original one, never went further than Francis Street corner, his whole life was spent between Bridgefoot Street, Meath Street, John's Lane Church and Francis Street corner. Apart from his own begging trade the dealers of Thomas Street, Meath Street and the Iveagh Market in Francis Street gave him pots of money. He lived in a coal shed in the Coombe. His next door neighbour was Mrs. Thomas (no relation). This Johnny Forty Coats is the one who had a face like Jesus Christ according to some old Dublin people. The last time I saw him was outside Meath Street Chapel. I used to pay a visit to the church each evening and the bold Johnny was always on sentry duty, 'Give us sixpence, give us sixpence.' One night he annoyed me. 'Look Johnny,' I said, 'I'll be coming to this church every evening and I can't afford to give you sixpence every time.' He looked at me and said, 'I'll tell you what to do sir. Give us the sixpence on a Monday night and for the rest of the week

51

go in the side door at the priest's house and you'll miss me.'

Hairy Lemon was always good for a chase and didn't seem to like his Dublin nickname. He swore like blue hell which made us call out Hairy Lemon dozens of times. We never jeered Shell Shock Joe. He walked all to one side like the town of Balbriggan. There were many shell shock people on the streets of Dublin in the late thirties. Somehow as kids we treated them with respect, as war heroes. There were two classes of shell shock people, the well-to-do officer type and the down-and-out soldier type. Another ex-British Army officer used to parade along Eden Quay effing and blinding everyone and everything in sight. Apparently he fell off his horse in India and struck his head against a rock.

The Bugler Dunne wasn't really the bugler at all. No, it was his father who was the bugler, but the son wore the father's red coat and medals. His haunt was Patrick Street and The Coombe. His claim to fame was that he was the King's Bugler at the Battle of Balaclava (the Charge of the Light Brigade). 'Into the valley of death rode the six hundred' — well, it seems that before they rode into the valley, the Bugler Dunne was ordered to sound the retreat, but he mixed up his sounds and blew the advance and charge, and the rest of the story is history, and the Bugler Dunne had medals by the bucket load to prove it.

Love Joy and Peace hated the rain — I saw him one wet day at the Ha'penny Bridge trying to dry the road. A dry day was his delight in order to follow his artistic ambitions. He drew a large shamrock nearly as wide as the road on Wellington Quay, then he coloured it orange, white and green and then inserted the words: Love Joy and Peace. He was a fine, handsome man who wore a haversack on his back with two flags sticking out of it, the tricolour and the blue flag of Dublin. He came from a wealthy Dublin family who were saddle and harness makers for generations.

The Lavender Woman who sat at the corner of College Green and Grafton Street seemed to like the good weather. Her cry was 'Lavender for your drawers mam, it will keep them cool in this sticky weather'.

I was coming down Thomas Court one evening, the sun was only splitting the trees. Sitting outside number five, the birthplace of James Stephens the writer, were two old men repairing an old umbrella. One man was all action at the spokes, the other man was holding the umbrella handle with his finger. They were the first umbrella men I'd seen since my childhood days. 'Any umbrellas, any umbrellas to fix today,' they even had a song about it and there was a fair few of them about when I was a child. There were lovely umbrella signs on Essex Quay and Nassau Street where they manufactured umbrellas. Anyhow, I stopped to chat to my umbrella man. 'He's from Leitrim,' said the one who was all action, 'and I'm from Wexford.' 'How's business,' I asked. 'Well,' said the action man, 'to tell you the truth sir, It'd be a damn sight better if it was raining.'

> Rain, rain, come down,
> I'll owe you half a crown.
>
> Damn the weather,
> Damn the weather.
>
> Rain, rain, go up,
> I'll owe you half a cup.

7

Janey Mack
Me Shirt is Black

NOW WASN'T THAT terrible advice to give the poor fella whose shirt was black with dirt. Go to bed and cover his head and don't get up till Monday. Between you and me it was pagan advice. What about Mass or Sunday service. Sure we all know that no matter how poorly we were clad during the weekdays we always had shoes and a clean shirt and jersey (or gansey) for Sunday morning, but it was only for Sunday morning.

I can still hear the mother's voice ringing in me ears, 'Get off that shirt and gansey and yer new shoes and put on yer rags'.

'Ah mammy, please, let's keep the shirt on.'

'Get it off before I brain yer, you're not going to play your gutter games in your good clothes.'

'I won't play games mammy I'll just walk around, ah please mammy.'

The mother wouldn't answer and her right hand would reach for the leather belt which was always hanging on the back door, but I never saw her take it down. In a flash I'd be up the stairs, muttering under my breath and dragging the gansey and new shirt off my back. At this rate of going the little shirt will last a lifetime. It wasn't the only shirt I had but it was the nicest one, royal blue with white pearl shirt buttons and it even had a little pocket on the chest. It was a better fitting shirt on my neck, and around my body and it

Janey Mack me shirt is black,
What will I do for Sunday?
Go to bed and cover yer head,
And don't get up till Monday.

hadn't got as long a tail as my other shirt. The tail of the other shirt was so long that it used to hang down the leg of my short trousers. Every kid in Inchicore would roar after me:

Hey you —
Dicky Dicky Dout
With his shirt sticking out,
Four yards in
And four yards out.

Now, as well as being a Dicky Dout meself I have seen a fair few Dicky Douts in my day.

The latest Dicky Dout I saw was sitting on the steps of Adam and Eve's Church, but he wasn't a kid he was an old man. He was sorting out all his treasures on the church steps. A bottle of wine half full, a handful of cigarette butts — which I suppose he collected in the gutter — a couple of ten-pence pieces and about twenty cuts of bread and butter. 'Would you have tenpence,' said he, 'so that I can buy a bit of bread.' I gave him a few bob and walked up Merchant's Quay with the verse Dicky Dicky Dout running in my mind with memories of shirts and Janey Macks.

At the top of Merchants' Quay I noticed a large crowd in O'Reilly's, the auctioneers. A big notice in the window told me it was an auction of soft goods or what's known in the pawn office trade as the sale of unredeemed pledges. As I walked in the door a bundle of coloured shirts were coming or going under the hammer. I spotted another notice on O'Reilly's wall which stated that a general sale would be held the following Monday at 7 p.m., and among the items of jewellery, watches, pens and china were historical books and Malton prints of old Dublin. Now I can understand a man pawning his shirt for a drink or the rent because I'd pawn my shirt any day to buy a historical book and a Malton print. I went to the auction and gave little signs to the auctioneer like the way the swanks do it at Sotheby's and I came home with two Malton prints and a large copy of the *London*

Illustrated News for the years 1853 and 1854. This was a great buy, a real gem studded with fascinating information about Dublin, Ireland, England and the World. The engravings alone were a masterpiece.

As I browsed through its pages I came across an engraving of Thomas Hood's memorial statue in Kensal Green Cemetery, and across the statue were written the words: 'He sang the song of a shirt'. Well now Thomas Hood wasn't the only one who sang the song of the shirt, I sang the song of the shirt meself, it was my party piece which I always gave as an encore after Peadar Kearney's 'Tri-coloured Ribbon'. I can only sing you the first verse because my aunt who taught me the song said that the second verse was vulgar.

> Oh, I'll never forget the day that I was born,
> It was upon a cold and frosty morn,
> The doctor said I looked a pretty chap
> And when the nurse she took me on her lap
> Oh she washed me all over I remember
> Powdered me so carefully you see
> It was a jolly good thing for me that I was wearing
> Oh the little shirt me mother made for me.

Now I don't know what way Mister Thomas Hood sang his song of the shirt but I sang my song with great gusto. Sure wasn't the song of the shirt my roots, my bread and 'Maggie Ryan' and my mother and my aunt's daily job.

The mother was a shirt maker and the aunt was a shirt examiner. The aunt checked the mother's shirts before they left the factory. All my shirts were home made and home examined before they went on my back. The mother even made shirts at home. Piece work, she called it, running up collars on the big, foot-operated Singer sewing machine which at one time belonged to my granny.

'How many did you make Alice,' my aunt would ask.

'Four and a half dozen, and the eyes are falling out of me head . . . Ah well, it's another seven shillings.'

Sometimes the aunt complained about the mother's shirt-making and the mother complained about the aunt's examining. 'She wouldn't know a well made shirt if it hit her in the face.' There was great sisterly love between them but it never stood in the way of examining shirts.

At the age of seven years I was a walking encyclopaedia on shirts and shirt making.

'There's Lily out of Somax she must have left Ferrier Pollocks, it's a wonder she never went to Faulats or Arnotts. McCrea's is the best of all,' me mother would say, 'I'd never leave Mister McCrea of Wood Street. Which reminds me Sarah' me mother would add, 'how old is Johnny Fox? I saw him this morning all dressed up in a new suit, lovely collar and tie and he only looked thirty.' 'The last time he saw thirty,' said the aunt, 'was on a hall door.' But Johnny Fox's age was forgotten. 'What colour shirt had he on . . . do you know the black stripe we're working on at the moment, well nearly the same as that only the stripe was thicker.'

Johnny Fox had his shop in Bride Street around the corner from Wood Street. The shop was a mountain of you-name-it in bike wheels, valves, bolts and nuts, washers, copper pipes, or, as the Dublin people said, 'Johnny Fox sells from a needle to an anchor. If you can't get it anywhere else try Johnny Fox.'

I'm wondering now where Johnny bought his shirt, was it one of me mother's, or was it a Kingston Shirt which 'Made All The Difference', or was it a 'Faulat Magic Cuff Shirt' with a double front? The magic cuff was two cuffs on each sleeve, when the first cuff got dirty you could turn it up and pull down the second cuff. The double fronts were like bullet-proof waistcoats. But they were the days when shirts were shirts. A grand long tail for comfort and three collars to every shirt, and if it was a white shirt, you could buy a spare semi-stiff glazed collar for only a bob. A Van Heusen spare collar was the London-made collar worn by kings, princes and dukes, and sold at a half dollar. You could also buy a 'dicky', which was a collar and front semi-stiff glazed under yer coat, and you wouldn't know the difference between a dicky and a shirt.

The only trouble with the loose collars were the studs. The back stud and the front stud were a holy terror, and if one of the studs fell under the bed it was murder. Getting some collars to meet around the neck with the two holes in the right places and the studs doing their job was often a work of art. If you pulled the front stud forward the back stud nearly bore a hole in the back of your neck. If you pulled the back stud forward you nearly swallowed yer Adam's apple. 'Where's me stud, who took the button hook?' 'Keep yer shirt on, I'm coming,' me mother would cry out.

And wasn't it funny that when shaving you always seemed to cut yourself in a place that put blood on the collar. The collars also had little matchstick-type bones to keep the points firm and straight. Sometimes these little bones went for a walk around the collar and it was another work of art getting them back in place.

There were two kinds of tie pins: one that went into your tie like a brooch and the other that held the two sides of the collar under your tie and fought a battle all night with yer Adam's apple. Cuff links were a must, these were another source of trouble. I think the cuff links thought their job was to escape rather than stay tied up to the shirt sleeve. Houdini was only in the ha'penny place to some cuff links I've had.

The war came, shirt material was scarce and the mother and aunt were on short time and shorter wages. During the war blackouts, the men were advised to walk in front of the ladies with their white shirt tails hanging out like Dicky Dicky Dout.

The war ended, shirt material became plentiful and now designs and fast colours took over the shirt trade: Janey Mack me shirt is pink or orange or lemon or even purple like the cloths that covered the church statues during Passion Week. Then came the 'drip-drys', long pointed collars, short stubby collars and shaped bodies which after a few washes makes one feel like the Incredible Hulk. The shirt box vanished to be replaced by a plastic bag.

There is nothing private about the shirt anymore. They are in the shops in rows and rows and everyone is taking

them up and putting them down. God be with the old days when you asked to see a white shirt and the assistant took down several boxes, opened the lids, pulled back the white tissue paper and let you look at the shirt in all its glory. Another thing — the lovely long tail for comfort has vanished — replaced by bum freezers.

There was a time in Dublin when you could tell what a man was by the colour of his shirt . . . oh God me judge you could . . . A man with a blue shirt was a policeman, a man with a red shirt was a communist, a man with a green shirt was a republican, a man in a khaki shirt was a British soldier, a man in a grey shirt was a Free State soldier, a man with a white shirt was a clerk, but a man in a white shirt with no collar was a farmer. A man with a black shirt was a gangster, or a spiv, who sold black market picture house tickets on a Sunday.

The men in James's Street with the striped hair shirts were always inmates of the South Dublin Union Workhouse.

Shirts today come in all shapes, sizes, colours, materials and prices, but gone are the days of a shirt for nine shillings and eleven pence and four ties for a ten shilling note.

I see in the Golden Pages that you can get your shirt repaired, altered or even made to measure. Do you remember yer man in D'Olier Street who used to turn your ol' suit inside out for twelve shillings? Well, take me tip if you are getting a shirt made to measure, add two foot to your height to ensure that you get a good old-fashioned tail to keep your bum warm. The other day I saw my father-in-law reading my *London Illustrated News.* As soon as he saw the Thomas Hood memorial he cried out, 'The song of the shirt, I remember it well in my school book seventy years ago, there was a picture, of a seamstress sitting at a window stitching a shirt. Wait now, he said, and then came the words:

> Stitch stitch stitch,
> In poverty hunger and dirt.
> Stitch stitch stitch,
> Mending the poor man's shirt.

8

The Ghost Season

THE GHOST SEASON started on Hallowe'en. 'Any apples an' nuts Missus?' and ended on Holy Thursday night in Stephen's Green after visiting the seven chapels. During the season we made broad daylight tours of all the haunted places. 'Janey, it's a spookey place, it gives me the creeps, I wouldn't like to be here after dark.'

Daytime visits weren't too bad, but at night-time we wouldn't go next to near them. We all knew where to avoid. The litany of ghosts and haunted places were whispered out with names and addresses as we sat around the huge bonfire on the banks of the Grand Canal roasting potatoes. Even the potatoes had ghosts. The Famine Lady who went around every night begging a potato. When someone went in to get her a potato she vanished. The Famine Lady dressed in old workhouse clothes with high laced brown boots and a calico bonnet. On All Souls' Night some women left potatoes and bread and milk outside the hall door for the poor souls who came from Purgatory for something to eat.

The game we played with our fists came from the Famine times.

> One potato,
> Two potato,
> Three potato,
> Four.

Somebody under the bed,
Whoever can it be.
I feel so very nervous
I call for Eileen.
Eileen lights the candle,
Nobody there.
Ee I Didly Die,
Out goes she.

Five potato,
Six potato,
Seven potato,
More.

The game went on putting our fists on top of all the other fists and counting potatoes. During the Famine the people begged for potatoes, and we with dozens of them around the bonfire. 'We will want to watch out that the Famine ghosts don't come back and haunt us for wasting potatoes.' So we ate the black roasted ones as well as the brown roasted ones for fear of the Famine ghosts.

The litany of ghosts started with Rialto Bridge. 'Don't go near Rialto Bridge, the Devil's Ghost appeared there in the shape of a black dog.' This had us looking out for dogs of any colour. 'Don't go down by the Robbers' Den and the Forty Steps, cos' it's loaded with the ghosts of all the people that the Highway men killed and robbed.' 'Every night the ghosts come back looking for their jewels and money that's buried in the Robbers' Den.' This one took us on daylight treasure tours, digging up the Robbers' Den, but we never found a make (ha'penny). 'Keep away from the Union Wall at Pigtown, the Dead Nun's Ghost comes through the wall at midnight.'

The litany went on: Robert Emmet's Ghost just beyond Harold's Cross Bridge. The Green Lady who walks on the waters of the Grand Canal, The Headless Horseman in Blackpitts in the Liberties. The Hunchback's Ghost who rides a horse along the Military Road at Goldenbridge. The Banshee who roams around every street and road at night-time, wailing and crying and combing her long hair. Every piece of broken comb was avoided like the plague. We kicked everything on the street, tin cans, stones, empty match boxes and cigarette boxes, but broken combs were left where the Banshee dropped them. Some of the combs had the teeth missing in the middle, this was a sign that the Banshee was angry.

All the graveyards were to be avoided as the dead got up

at night for a bit of a walk. Goldenbridge and the Bullys' Acre were the two nearest graveyards to us. There wasn't much talk about Goldenbridge but Bullys' Acre was the chief fear of our childhood. 'That's where the bodies were dug up every night and sold to the College of Surgeons in Stephen's Green.' 'Only those that didn't get up for a walk, were dug up and sold.' The other dead bodies went for their ghostly walks along the John's Road. Walking home from town at night-time everyone avoided the John's Road and came the long way home by the Conyngham Road and Island Bridge Barracks.

After the litany of ghosts and haunted places, someone's mother had heard the Banshee's cry and the mother knew there was going to be a death in the neighbourhood soon. A few days later, black crepe and a card appeared on a door. In those days most people died in their own homes and nearly every week there was a death. The wakes were powerful for lemonade and doughnuts, but visiting the corpse was a terror. As soon as the crepe appeared, we ran to St. Michael's Church and did the Stations of the Cross for the dead person. Then we ran back to the house of the dead to give our sympathy and tell of our prayers.

'He's upstairs,' the woman would say, and 'yis are very good boys.'

We climbed the stairs very slowly. Sometimes there might be a few people in the room with the dead person, having a chat as if he wasn't there at all. Other times the room would be empty with only the dead man and us. The corpse lay on the all white bed in a brown habit with his hands joined and a pair of rosary beads in his fingers. All the mirrors in the room were covered with white sheets. The first thing we did was to sprinkle holy water on the corpse with a small piece of palm. A little table by the bedside had what was known as a Sick Call Set. The set consisted of a crucifix, a pair of candlesticks in which two holy candles burned, and a small bowl of holy water and a sprig of palm. Some people kissed the corpse for affection or to save them from dreaming of the corpse. We never went that far, we took our chance on the

65

dreams. After shaking the holy water, we knelt down and said three Hail Marys very quickly with our eyes closed. Then we went down to the kitchen for the lemonade and cakes.

The following night the corpse was carried to the church at eight o'clock. This gave everyone a chance to show their respect for the dead and in carrying the coffin, the expense of having the hearse and mourning coaches were saved. More expense was saved by everyone who was going to the funeral, paying their own shilling for a seat in a horse cab. It was seven shillings a cab to the graveyard and back, the cabs held six people inside and one up on the dicky beside the driver. We went to the funeral by scutting on the back of the cabs, and on the way home we got more lemonade and ginger snap biscuits at the 'Brian Boru' sent out to us by the 'corpse's brother'.

After the Banshee stories, someone's ould fella had heard footsteps following him and weird sounds as he made his way home from night work. He was coming along by Old Kilmainham when he heard footsteps behind him. He turned around, and at this stage in the story someone would grab me from behind and say, 'He has yeh. He has yeh' and I nearly died of fright. The footsteps stopped, he started again and the footsteps started again. The stopping and starting kept going on until he reached Kerin's Place, then he started to run, the footsteps started to run, the sweat was pouring off him as he ran and he was as white as a sheet. The ould fella's wife said that 'It must have been the ghost of the Old Kilmainham Jail at Watery Lane. The prisoner who was shot dead while trying to escape.'

The Green Lady walks along the waters of the Grand Canal at eleven o'clock every night. As soon as we heard this, we all asked the time. 'Mister, what time is it? Is it near eleven?' We were always afraid to go home in case the ghosts, or Banshee or Green Ladies were waiting to grab us.

One night we heard strange noises in the canal. 'It must be the Green Lady' said a voice. There was a scatter down Kickham Road quicker than any race. Another night we got very brave, we all armed ourselves with sticks and stones and a few iron bars and we were going to wait for the Green Lady. Everyone's knees were knocking but no one budged from the canal bank. We heard the noise, and still we waited, the noise came nearer and nearer and then a swan jumped up on the bank. 'It's only a . . .? Janey, she's changed herself into a swan.' We were all familiar with the story of the Children of Lir. Children changing into swans is one thing but ould Green Ladies changing into swans is something else. There was another scatter down the road and from that night onwards we were always very wary of swans. The only safe ghost in Dublin was the Soldier's Ghost in the sentry box high up on the side wall of Kilmainham Jail. He had no ladder and he couldn't get down to grab you, he was also a daytime and a night-time ghost. They forgot to change the guard and the soldier died in the sentry box. We never went to see the ghost at night-time but we saw it millions of times during the day. As well as the real thing in ghosts, there were always a good few 'letty on ones'. Kids dressing up in old white sheets and waiting at dark corners and up the back passage of the houses to come out quickly and scare the wits out of us.

The only time we weren't afraid of ghosts was when we were waiting in Stephen's Green on Holy Thursday to see the sign of the cross in the window of Iveagh House. This was where the Green Lady lived, or so we thought. Standing with us was all Dublin and its mother. After visiting the seven chapels, the crowds came from every direction to Stephen's Green. There were many stories of how the cross came into the window on Holy Thursday. Some said that the Green Lady jumped out of the window to her death because she wasn't allowed to say the rosary on Holy Thursday. The Green Lady spent her time walking on the canal water and putting her cross in the window on Holy Thursday. Maybe, as well as seeing the cross, we'll see her jumping out of the window. Despite all the people shouting that they could see the cross I could see nothing. We went home disgusted, the Green Lady was a fraud. Still, Holy Thursday after Holy

Thursday, we went to Stephen's Green. My last visit to the house of the Green Lady to see the sign of the cross was in my early teenage years. Me and my pal were looking up at the window, when this pretty young wan shouted out that she could see the cross. Then me pal shouted out that he could see it. There they were, the pretty mot and me pal seeing the cross and I could see nothing. I was bleary eyed looking, but still I saw nothing. On the way home that night I said to me pal 'Did you really see the cross?'

'No,' he said. 'I saw nothing.'

'Then why did you say you saw it?' I asked.

'Well,' he said, 'when the pretty mot said she saw it, she held me hand.'

'She had a lovely hand and I was afraid that if I didn't say I saw it she'd let go, and besides I've a date with her for Easter Saturday.'

Well out looking for ghosts and strange signs is one thing, but picking up a pretty mot at the same time is something else.

'I hope she wasn't the Banshee's daughter,' I said.

69

9

Jembo No Toes

WELL, YER MAN Holy Moses wasn't the only one to shout. Me mother and me granny let out a quare few shouts in their day over shoes and boots. 'My God, will ya look at them,' mother would say, 'two big holes in the soles and down on the heels as well. Leather isn't the same now as it was years ago or are the waxies using cardboard to make boots and shoes?' Now cardboard was the stuff that we used to use in our boots as inside soles or to cover a hole in the sides to keep out the wet. But rainwater would bore a hole in an iron pot, my granny said, and it wasn't too long before the cardboard became soggy socks that made the feet squeak like mice. A hole in the sole was bad enough, but to be down on the heel as well was the lower half of the barrel. The shoemaker's shop in Dorset Street spelt it out in large red letters:

DON'T PASS THIS SHOP
AND HAVE THAT FEEL
THAT YOU ARE DOWN ON THE HEEL

Shoemakers' shops everywhere warned of the dangers of unprotected feet. Mr. Lynch of Francis Street and Mr. Barnwell of Castle Street, whose forefathers had been shoemakers for generations, had their shop windows full of signs.

Holy Moses, King of the Jews,
Bought his wife a pair of shoes.
When the shoes began to wear,
Holy Moses began to swear.
When the shoes were quite worn out,
Holy Moses began to shout.

Well done Cobler

We sole the living
Not the dead.
We are the doctors
Of the leather and thread.

'Don't risk cold and 'flu, have your boots properly mended today . . . Double the life of your boots, stick a sole on today.' Now this was a second sole to give the first sole better protection. Rimforts or Phillips stick a sole. But Phillips were rubber soles and heels and everyone said that rubber was bad for yer feet and made yeh blind. That's why some shoemakers' signs said, 'Leather for Health'. I don't know if rubber soles and heels made you blind but I do know that them clogs and platform shoes that youngwans wear make yeh deaf. And that if yer mot wears stiletto heals to a dance ye'll need a fine pair of shinguards.

I wonder did St. Crispin, the patron saint of shoemakers, ever let a shout at the type of shoe or boot that was made by shoemakers? Hush Puppies, Doc Martins, cowboy boots, desert boots and them pointed-toe shoes that made us look like Ali Baba in Baghdad. I'm sure St. Patrick's face was red when the shoemakers of Dublin started to make the reptile shoes for ladies. Then some bright shoemaker added croco-dile shoes. Then the ladies had crocodile handbags and croco-dile raincoats. Did you ever make a date with a mot dressed like a crocodile? In our childhood days the shoe and boot fashion didn't change all that much. We had Little Duke black boots. Brown boots were reserved for countrymen to fit in with their blue serge suits, canary yellow pullovers and brown tweed caps. In the winter we had a pair of wellington boots, but the wellies made our feet sweat. Then another bright spark came along with a cure for smelly feet, the magic inside sole that eats up the smell.

In the summer time we wore brown sandals but the straps always broke. The most popular thing in summer for the feet was a pair of white runners. Runners came in three colours, black, brown and white. The white runners got dirty very very quickly, so every Saturday night we had to make a saucerful of Blanco. It was sold in square boxes and looked like a square piece of white chalk. It was about the size of a twenty packet of cigarettes. We scraped the Blanco with a knife on to the saucer, added water and made a watery white paste. This was applied to the white runners with a piece of cloth. The paste took about twelve hours to dry, so the runners were left out on the window-sill overnight. Sunday morning the runners would be white as snow. The trouble only started when I put on the runners. Every step I took on me way to Mass sent up a white cloud of Blanco. When I got to the chapel the runners were back to their pre-Blanco colour.

Blanco was a household name. It was also used by soldiers to clean their Webb belting. I knew a soldier who used to use a lot of Blanco and he always said that if he found himself facing an enemy without his rifle that he'd shake himself and blind the enemy with Blanco. In those days soldiers wore leather leggings and leather bandoliers and the best turned out soldier I ever saw was an artillery man named Mullins of Devoy Road. With his boots, leggings and bandolier shining, he looked a sight for sore eyes. The general, we used to call him, though he didn't like the rank we gave him. But despite our childhood jeers we all had great admiration for his neatness and style.

What a contrast he was to poor old Jembo No Toes, the blind artillery man of the Liberties. He was called 'no toes' because he had bad feet and he used to cut the toe caps out of his boots. I can see him now coming up Patrick Street, the toes sticking out through the top of his boots and he singing his signature song.

> I don't want to go to the trenches no more
> Where the alley man's guns shatter and roar.
> Omy ome, Take me home over the sea,
> Back to the Liberties.

And going down the far side of the street is Soodlum, the man who only wore ammunition boots or gun boots,

73

military boots as other people called them. 'Excuse me, sir, would you have a pair of ammunition boots . . . Meself and Cromwell are the only two men in the world who never slept in the same bed twice . . . Ammunition boots, sir, have yeh a spare pair of ammunition boots?' When Soodlum met young ladies he forgot about his ammunition boots and instead he'd put his hand into his coat pocket and ask the ladies, 'Will I take it out for you?' The poor ladies, not knowing what was to come out, ran like hell down Patrick Street, and sure all poor ol' Soodlum took out was a tin whistle. 'Will I take it out for you, miss . . . excuse me, sir, would you have a spare pair of ammunition boots?'

'Excuse me, mister, me mother said you could show me another pair of them Little Duke boots at a cheaper price?' The man in Frawleys shop raised his eyes to heaven and once more went up the ladder to add yet another shoebox to the mountain of shoe boxes on the counter. The mother looked at the price on the box. 'Come on,' she said to me, 'thank you, but I'll try somewhere else,' said me mother as she walked out of the shop. I was still lacing me old boots under the counter, so the man in Frawleys didn't see me. He mimicked my mother, 'Thank you, but I'll try somewhere else, yeh silly ol' bitch, look at all the boots I've to put back on the shelf.' As I rose up from under the counter I mimicked him and ended up with you silly ol' so and so. But after all he had a point. Buying a pair of boots or shoes today is not like it was in my childhood days. When I was a kid buying a pair of boots was like a day's outing — the soft chair to sit on, the footrest, the shopman's shoe horn, and, if you bought a pair of boots, they were either left in the box or you could put your old ones into the box and wear the new ones home. But you always got a shoebox and if you met anyone on the way home, they always knew that you were after buying a pair of shoes. The shoebox was a status symbol, and I've seen shoeboxes used for all sorts of things. They were used as button boxes, cigarette picture boxes, wool boxes, dolls' beds and magic boxes. A magic box was made out of a shoebox by putting holes in the top of the box and sticking different coloured sweet papers into the holes. The inside of the box was lined with old Christmas cards and a peep hole was cut at one end of the box. We charged five cigarette pictures for a look in the magic box, with a verse of

> Roll up roll up
> And see the magic show
> A lady on the poe.

We usually had a queue to see the magic shoebox.

Nowadays when you buy a pair of shoes you have to do a balance act while you try one on. Shoes are in shop windows and on shelves like apples and oranges, and if you find a shoe to fit you, the assistant has to make a search to find the other shoe and then they are wrapped up like a Ringsend ray or a few kippers.

Whenever we were in town as kids we used to love to watch the posh kids coming out of Bradley's shoe shop in Nassau Street. Bradleys not only gave a good shoebox but they gave each child a balloon as well. A free balloon, a big one on a stick in colours red, blue and green, with 'Buy Bradley's Shoes' written on it. As a child I used to think that Bradley's was the best shoe shop in the world. But we only got as far as Frawleys, Duffys and Guineys and they never gave us balloons. Guiney's green paper was better known than Nelson's Pillar, but it was a poor substitute for a balloon.

Whenever I moaned about boots or shoes the ma would always say, 'What about the poor children with no boots?' There were thousands of bare-footed children in my day and the Herald Boot Fund did a fine job in trying to remedy this evil, but I remember kids whose fathers were in fair jobs and who always wore boots, being sent to school in their bare feet the day the free Herald boots were being given out. To prevent these boots ending up in the pawn shop the boots were stamped H.B.F. on the soles. Some bright spark discovered that a red hot poker could remove the H.B.F.

and some of the boots ended up in the pawn while the children ran bare-footed around Dublin. If the pawn money was used for food God bless them that did it. I never got a pair of the H.B.F. boots because no matter how broken my boots were I was never sent to school in the bare feet.

I remember going to work in the laundry on a very wet day. My mother ran after me down the South Circular Road and made me change my broken boots for a pair of my sister's shoes. I did not like the idea of wearing girls' shoes, but my mother insisted, 'Wet feet will give you your end' (death), she said, 'and no one will notice the shoes in the rain.' So I gave her the broken boots and went to work in my sister's shoes. They seemed to fit all right but were a little tight across the toes. The rain never let up. It was coming down like cats and dogs. I was drowned as I wandered down Dollymount Avenue collecting dirty laundry. Suddenly my two feet burned with pain. It was as if they were being pressed in an iron vice. I kicked off the shoes and pressed the pain out of my toes. My real trouble started when I tried to put the shoes back on — my feet wouldn't go into them. I was like the ugly sisters with Cinderella's shoe. So I ended up putting the shoes in my pocket and walking around Clontarf in my stocking feet. All during the day I tried several times to get the shoes back on but I failed every time. My only consolation was that I found a lovely bit of hard cardboard sticking out of an ashbin in Haddon Road. This piece of cardboard would cover the broken soles in me old boots. I'll never forget that night when I came home. The first thing I saw as I came into the kitchen was me old boots newly mended, covered with steel studs, steel heel-tips and steel toe-tips. Mr. Coughlan, our good neighbour who was a shoemaker in the army in Clancy Barracks, was after doing a special job on me old boots.

When boot laces broke we used twine with a dash of boot polish. One morning in Switzers I was stopped by the manager, Mr. Warren. He looked down at my boots and saw my twine laces. 'Do you sweep the shoe department?' he asked. 'I do, sir,' I said. 'Well,' said he, 'could you not knock off a pair of bootlaces for yerself?' I blushed. 'Go back,' said he, 'and with my permission treat yourself to a pair of bootlaces.' As I went back to get the laces I couldn't help thinking, 'It's a pity I didn't meet you on Dollymount Avenue.'

Shoes have always been a status symbol. How many times have you heard people say, 'God love him, he hadn't a shoe on him . . . He was down on the heel . . . He's not fit to clean your boots.' I love the story of the poet who instead of getting twenty-five horses for his beautiful poems was given instead a pair of boots, an insult to the Gaelic poet meaning he hadn't a boot on him. The poet took the pair of boots, held them up high and made a beautiful poem on the boots.

> The leather for these boots
> Came from the white bull of Cooley.
> They were worn by Alexander the Great,
> They were worn by Brian at Clontarf,
> They are rugged to wear against the stones
> As I go on my travels.
> They are soft inside for comfort,
> There is something of my own character in them.

With this tradition it's no surprise that we all got the lesson of writing in school the autobiography of an old boot.

The shoemakers and shoe-repairers of today follow a noble tradition that is nearly as old as Dublin itself. In the early days of our city they followed their trades in Shoemaker Lane which is today known as Ross Road in the Liberties. Their patron saint may be St. Crispin, but their ancient guild which dates from 1427 was under the protection of Blessed Mary and St. Michael the Archangel. Their work in Shoemaker Lane was also under the watchful eye of St. Werburgh, St. Martin, St. Nicholas and St. Bride whose churches were on the shoemakers' doorsteps. When the shoe-makers came out to parade on Corpus Christi or to ride the fringes, they carried a banner of St. Crispin and their flag colours were red, blue and green, like Bradley's balloons.

10

Red Carbolic and Yellow Sunlight

THE BEAUTY OF DUBLIN WIT and thinking is that when something goes wrong, there's always something better on the way. Like the washing girl, whose fella didn't turn up to help her with the washing, so to hell with him, he needn't come no more, she'll get the Prince of Wales. The old people have a lovely way of putting this thinking, 'God never shut one door but He opened a half dozen'. There isn't as much folklore singing in Dublin today as there was in my childhood. Every wash day in our house was like a ballad session. The clothes were hand scrubbed to the airs of 'Napper Tandy' and the 'Boys of Wexford'. Monday was wash day, the kitchen, where the washing took place, was out of bounds to children. To enforce that rule, a kitchen chair was put on its side to block the entrance. Wash day began by getting out the big black iron pots that were only used at Christmas time and on washing days. These were filled with cold water and put on the gas to boil. There was no hot water in the taps in my childhood. The 'geezer' came much later.

The 'geezer' was the Gas Company water heaters, which were supplied at sixpence a week. A geezer was also the nickname or slang word for a cat. A woman was complaining one time, about the trouble she had trying to heat the washing water. 'Why don't you get a 'geezer', said me Ma. 'Sure what would I be doing with a cat?' said she, 'and me with two dogs'. The four gas jets were always going full blast

78

Monday is me washing day,
Tuesday I'm alone,
Wednesday is me ironing day,
I hope me fella comes.
He didn't come last Wednesday,
Nor the Wednesday before
And if he doesn't come this Wednesday
He needn't come no more.

The dirty old thing, he didn't come,
He didn't come, he didn't come.
The dirty old thing, he didn't come
To help me with me washing.
So now, I'll get the Prince of Wales,
The Prince of Wales, the Prince of Wales,
So now I'll get the Prince of Wales
To help me with me washing.

under the black pots, sometimes I'd get the call to put another tuppence in the gas. The gas meter was the penny type, it was in the closet or coal house as we called it. It was always pitch dark and it was nearly a work of art to get the penny into the slot and twist the knob on the first go. When the water was boiled, it was poured into a big galvanised bath, which was sitting on two kitchen chairs. The first thing put into the water was washing soda. This was to make the water soft. The washing soda was sold in black sugar bags, it was three ha'pence for a two pound bag and it looked like dirty hard ice. It lasted for about four wash days. The next thing to be added to the water was a penny ball of Reckitt's Blue. The Blue was for bringing out the white in the shirts, sheets and pillowcases. The Blue was also used for wasp or bee stings. There were no washing powders, Rinso and Persil were for the swank. The nearest we got to Rinso was the street folklore song for girls, which they sang while playing with a ball.

Plainy a packet of Rinso,
Over a packet of Rinso,
Downy a packet of Rinso,
Dashy a packet of Rinso,
Right leg a packet of Rinso,
Left leg a packet of Rinso,
Belly a packet of Rinso,
Backy a packet of Rinso.

Note, it was never 'Washy' a packet of Rinso.

On the old Persil packets there were two boys, one in a grey-white shirt and the other in a snow-white shirt with the caption, 'Someone's Mother isn't using Persil'. Anyone appearing in a dirty shirt was reminded that their mother wasn't using Persil. The clothes were steeped in the water, washing soda and blue and they were left for a while to allow the water to cool down. The washing board was placed in position in the bath and the half pound of Sunlight Soap was firmly held in my aunt's left hand. Up onto the washing board came the clothing to be rubbed and rubbed and rubbed with the Sunlight Soap. In next to no time the bath would be a giant ball of suds. Sometimes we used red carbolic soap, the black soap was used for washing the floors, we washed ourselves in yellow Sunlight. The soap was sold in pound and two half-pound bars. It was packed in one pound bars and was cut with a piece of twine. Some shops had the soap twine nailed to the counter. Sunlight Chambers in Parliament Street was at one time the head office of Barringtons, Creans and Levers, the soap manufacturers. The beautiful two-tier frieze around the building depicts people working and dirtying their clothes and women drawing water and washing clothes and, of course, using soap.

After three hours of washing and singing we were allowed into the kitchen to fill tin mugs with the soapy water for blowing soap bubbles with a white penny clay pipe. More water was boiled for the rinse. Then, the mangle came out of the shed in the back yard. Our mangle looked as if it came out of the Ark with Noah. Nevertheless, it did the job. The clothes-lines were prepared with pegs and the hanging up job began with prayers for no rain. The airing of the clothes was done around the fire. The bloomers and ladies underwear were hung under the mantlepiece cloth and out of view. The ironing was next. No wonder yer man in the verse didn't turn up. Watching the ironing was a very boring job, the only excitement was the heating and testing of the iron. The iron was heated at the fire or on the gas, testing was done by spitting on the iron and watching the little white snowballs roll off the iron into the fire-grate. I never saw anything being scorched or burned. The iron had to be heated several times.

Washday began at nine o'clock and finished at two o'clock and then the job of making the dinner began. The aunt's hands and arms would be roaring red from the soda and hot water and her nails were as white as snow. Washerwomen never needed manicures. Starching and home dyeing were only done on special occasions. Red Robin Starch came in thru'penny packets. It was like little balls of chalk. Starching was done separately in the small basin. Glazing it was called by the old people. Collars, cuffs and dicky fronts were all starched. I used to think that the French Sisters of Charity with their big turned up white starched hats and shining white bibs were the best starchers in Dublin. Drummer dyes were sold in little glass containers about the size of a tube of lipstick, at sixpence each. When a death took place in a family, all the women's clothes were dyed black. The men wore black ties, black armbands or black diamond-shape patches sewn on the sleeve of their coats. White hankies had a black border all around them. People in mourning wore the black clothes for twelve months and during that time had no entertainment of any kind.

We have come a long way from the five hours washing on a Monday to the automatic washing machines and spin dryers of today. Did you ever stop to think how it all started? Whenever you use your washing machine give a thought to the Magdalen idea, the idea which set in motion the first organised laundry. The laundry idea led to laundry engineering, which in turn led to your washing machine. On a bleak windy day in March 1751, as a Londoner was passing by a foundling hospital and watching the children, his thoughts turned to their unhappy mothers. He went home and wrote a letter to the *Rambler* magazine. He signed the letter 'Amicus'. This letter led to the founding of the Magdalen Hospital in 1758. Robert Dingley set out his plans for establishing a public place of reception for penitent prostitutes. Part of the plan was for the employment of inmates.

The first Magdalen House opened in the old building of the London Hospital in Goodman's Field beside the Tenter Ground, where the cloth makers stretched their fabrics on tenter hooks. Seven years later Lady Arabella Denny founded the Magdalen Asylum at 8 Lower Leeson Street. Lady Denny was born in Lixnaw Castle, Tralee, County Kerry. Her whole life was devoted to charity, she spent her time, energy and money on behalf of the poor of Dublin. She presented a grandfather clock to the Foundling Hospital in the South Dublin Workhouse in James's Street. The inscription on the brass plate read: 'For the benefit of Infants, protected by this hospital, Lady Arabella Denny presents this clock to mark that as children reared by the spoon must have but a small quantity of food at a time, it must be offered frequently, for which purpose this clock strikes every twenty minutes, at which notice all ye Infants that are not asleep must be discreetly fed.' The employment given to the inmates of the Magdalen House was the washing, ironing, glazing, and sewing of clothes. But, whose clothes? The poor all washed their own clothes. The rich had their own laundries in their own homes. Who, then, will the Magdalens wash for? For gentlemen staying in hotels, who have to stay in Dublin longer than they expected, and who need clean shirts. All the hotels had notices of the washing services and business started to boom. St. Mary Magdalen's Asylum, Donnybrook, was founded by Mrs. Ryan in 1798 and was placed under the care of the Sisters of Charity. The Magdalen Asylum, 72 Lower Gloucester Street, was founded by the Reverend Father John Holmes in 1822. In my laundry days with the White Heather Laundry, the big horse vans of the High Park and Gloucester Street Laundries were a familiar sight in the streets of Dublin. In the early days all laundries were under the control of Magdalen Houses and convents. Every day John Hogg, who lived in 6 Upper Gloucester Street, used to see the loads of washing going into the Gloucester Laundry. Pots of money, he used to say to himself. In 1870 John Hogg started one of the first private laundries in his own house. He was soon followed by Mary Hague of 29 Aungier Street, The Manor Mill, Dundrum, Edmondstown Model Laundry, Rathfarnham, and Joe Beggs of the Dodder Bank. They were well known as Laundry Keepers. Well, at least, Joe Beggs hadn't far to go for water. Was your shirt ever washed in the Dodder River? Mine was, the day I fell in while catching pinkeens.

Mary Lynch started the Express Laundry in Marlboro' Street in 1876. She advertised in all the daily papers, 'Express Laundry — thirty hands. No chemicals used. The only cleansing agents used are pure soap and pure water and these, applied by the vigorous arms of herself and her assistants, quickly expel the dirt and give to the articles their new appearance.'

> Down by the Liffey where the green grass grows,
> Where Mary Lynch washes her clothes,
> She sang and she sang and she sang so sweet
> And she sang for her sweetheart up the street.
> Sweetheart, sweetheart, will you marry me?
> Yes love, yes love, at half past three.
> Ice cake, jam tarts, all for tea,
> And we're going to have the wedding at the D.B.C.*

*D.B.C. was Dublin Bread Company, Stephen's Green.

11

Hoops, Culchies and Jackeens

I'VE KNOWN MOLLYS with bikes, Mollys with skates, Mollys with foot scooters and men who claimed that they were in the 'Molly Maguires'. I've even bought Mollies from ould wans in Cork city, but never in me life did I ever meet a Molly with a hoop. In fact, in my day, hoops were strictly for boys. Oh! I often gave many's the mot a go on me hoop in exchange for the butt of her apple or the loan of her *Film Fun* comic. Now maybe that's an eighteenth century piece of Dublin street folklore, and maybe yer man wanted to roll the hoop of Molly's dress down by Smock Alley.

When Mister Handel came to Dublin in 1741, he took lodgings in Abbey Street. They say it was there that he put the finishing touches to his new work, *The Messiah*. He went to the organ in St. Michan's Church and played it to himself. Then, he decided to give the first performance of *The Messiah* in public for charity. 'What charity?' they asked. 'The Prison Gate Fund and the Prisoners' Dependents' answered Mr. Handel.

There were 'hims and haws', coughs and splutters and smelling salts passed around. The idea, the nerve, so a few other charitable organisations were added, including Mercer's Hospital. The posters went up all over Dublin. '*The Messiah* to be performed in the Fishamble Street Music Hall on April 13th 1742. Gentlemen are requested not to carry swords. Ladies, please leave your dress hoops at home.' Well, they all

Molly, I'd love to be rolling your hoop,
Rolling your hoop, rolling your hoop.
Molly, I'd love to be rolling your hoop
Down by the country gardens.

obeyed and they were packed in like sardines. When the performance ended a man stood up and shouted, 'Bravo, Bravo,' and this was the start of the 'standing ovation' in Dublin. When *The Messiah* went to London a few months later, the King followed the Dublin fashion and stood up to cheer. Now, more than likely, if the ladies had been wearing their dress hoops, the standing ovation might never have started.

I wonder did the game of hoops start with ladies' dress hoops in the eighteenth century? Hoops came in all sorts of shades and colours. In our day the most popular hoop was an old rusty bicycle wheel rim with no spokes. A fella with spokes in his hoop was a real swank and a fella with spokes in his hoop and a rubber tyre, well he was a snob. A good hoop would last a boy's lifetime. They were washed in the canal, the Camac, the Poddle, but they were never painted. We went everywhere with the hoops. The hoop stick acted as an accelerator and brake. Hoop races were more popular than bullseyes. Another type of hoop was the motor car tyre. We sat in this type of hoop and went down Kilmainham Hill forty times a day, nearly quicker than the trams. A push start, a good roll, but no brakes, so that the tyre ended up hitting a wall or the kerb of the footpath. But we never minded as the tough rubber always took the bumps. When we got fed up rolling the rubber hoop, we made a bonfire out of it on the banks of the Grand Canal.

So much for hoops, but what about the country gardens. Where in Dublin were the nearest country gardens. The nearest I was ever to the country in Dublin was up at Cow Town, the cattle market on the North Circular Road. Thursdays were great days. Prussia Street and Aughrim Street smelt like Old MacDonald's Farm. Market day, the coming and going of men, women, boys, girls and beasts. Every kid with a stick learning the trade of the shepherd and the cattle drover. Cows, bulls, sheep dogs, horses, mooing, baahing, shouting, spitting on hands and slapping, plenty of free milk and loads of cowshit. The more money the farmers had, the poorer they were dressed. They all wore old clothes and had their trousers tied at the knees with pieces of rope. And, the money, the likes of it we never saw before, red notes, brown notes, blue notes and big white notes, fistfulls of it and the pubs were doing a roaring trade. 'Mister, will I mind yer cows?' We never got any work or any money. Free milk, yes, and we with no jugs or bottles.

Every dairy shop in Dublin was like a little bit of the country. The smell of fresh buttermilk, the big white bowls of milk with muslin cloths to keep out the Dublin house flies, the 56 pound blocks of butter and the wooden butter knives standing in a tall delph jug with ice cool water. The marble top counters and shelves and the cat sipping in the window. The sign of the cat was the sign of fresh milk and a decent dairy woman. It was like magic, the way the butter knives cut into the big blocks of butter and took out the right amount and weighed it on the round white marble scales with shining brass weights. Then the butter was slapped about with the knives and made into the shape of a square box. The final touch came when the little lines of the butter knives left their mark on the butter. Every dairy had, at least, three dairy boys, the boys were over seventy years of age. They milked the cows and delivered the milk on bicycles. The dairy girls were a few years younger. Mary Gartlin was a dairy girl, she milked the cows in Goldenbridge Farm and delivered the milk all around Inchicore and Kilmainham. She'd fly down the Emmet Road like Stanley Woods, the motor bike racer, with three big cans of milk on the handle bars of her bike. She never needed a bell as the pint, half pint, and tilly measures rattled against the milk cans. The tilly was a little extra free milk, a sup for the cat.

I suppose, too, the country in Dublin, was in the form of the Church, the bank, the law, canal horses, Guiney's and education. Our parish priest was from County Kildare, the bank manager, not that we needed him, was a Sligo man, the local sergeant of police was a Mayo man. The canal horses always looked happier when they were heading towards the country than when they were coming into Dublin. Were they dreaming of open fresh country fields, the fragrance of newborn hay and a wind that would blow the flies and cool their tether?

Denis Guiney, where we got all our clothes, was a Kerry man, and all the school teachers were culchies. I saw a right digging match outside the GPO one Saturday night. 'What's up?' I asked.

'I'll tell ya what's up' answered this Dub. 'That bunch of Culchies called us "Jackeens".'

'Well, they didn't call us "Jackeens" when we saved the harvest for them,' said I.

'That's right,' said the Dub. 'Aten bread is soon forgotten.' Then, he started shouting at the Culchies. 'Have yis forgotten when we Jackeens saved the harvest for yis? Bedad we did. July 1943, Sluagh na Talmhan, 1000 Dublin volunteers wanted to save the harvest. Free holidays in the fresh country air, wholesome food, plenty of country sport. Apply, the Runaí, 28 Upper O'Connell Street.'

Well, we didn't have to apply. We drove down in Switzer's lorry every day. Trim, Tara, Maynooth, Ratoath, you name the farm and we Dubliners saved their harvest. The grub was great, the work was brutal, but we liked the country sport best of all. Before it was over, we all had country mots, fine big agricultural girls, some of them twice as big as us little Dubs. But the country mots didn't mind at all. They were all terrible sorry when the harvest was saved and made us promise to write to them. We were praying for another bad year to get back to the country harvest and sport. Well, for weeks after we did nothing but talk of the country mots, marry a country girl was our advice. No fancy notions like some of the Dublin gold-diggers. The turkey and goose at Christmas time, the summer holidays for yerself and the kids, and the odd bag of spuds and lorry load of turf or logs. But what about the All-Ireland finals, some asked, when they all come up from the country and ate ya out of house and home. Well, ya could always marry a girl from Clare, they were never in the finals.

One time, we were all day dreaming about the nicest sight in the world. This Clareman stood up and said, 'The nicest sight in the world would be to see the Clare hurling team following the Artane Band around Croke Park and the band playing "Clare's Dragoons". I wouldn't care,' he said, 'if they won or lost as long as they got to Croker for the final.' To us in teenage days, the finals always meant the night before the Big Match. We all went into town, O'Connell Street, and bought colours, gollywog hats and 'let on' we were up for the Match. Sometimes we were Kerrymen, and sometimes we were Galway men or Wexford men, the toss of a coin decided our county. Then we'd walk up and down O'Connell Street on both sides twenty times, clicking the mots. Some of the mots we fooled, but others were not taken in so easy by our Kerry accents. I remember one youngwan in Caffollas Ice Cream Parlour, looking over at us eating our Chocolate Flips and saying, 'Hey, you with the hats, you'se is not from Kerry, you'se is Dublin. Kerry me eye, gollywog hats don't fool me, you'se is as Dublin as the Coombe'. Not only did she blow our country cover to her pals, she blew it all over Caffollas and she was waiting in O'Connell Street when we came out. I think that was the last time we bought country colours and gollywogs. 'Oh! Heffo, oh! Jimmy Keaveney, oh! Paddy Cullen, where were yis when we were young?

Well, whatever about country girls and country men, the country in Dublin, you must admit that the country writers and poets have it far and above and better than us Dubs. They are never stuck for a line, a word, a verse or a sonnet. Sure it's no wonder that Yeats left Sandymount for Sligo. Evenings full of linnets' wings, golden countryside, purple and white heather, speckled lakes, jumping trout and wind blown flies, and mountainy men reaping near to the Gate of Heaven. We, in Dublin, haven't even a lake, unless you allow me to mention the Dog Pond up in the Park. Now, every real Dubliner knows the Dog Pond, but the country fella up working in the Ordnance Survey Depot making out his map of the Phoenix Park, what does he call it? The Citadel Pond. You see, everything in the country is different. Even the wind and rain is different. In Dublin, it's bloody well lashing cats and dogs and the wind would only skin you at Baggot

Street Bridge. But in the country it's a fine soft morning with the rain falling like silver pearls on the green arrow spikes of wild nettle leaves. And the wind plays a symphony of sweet music on a wire fence in Paddy Kavanagh's country. And what about the boglands? Where will you find golden brown turf in Dublin? Don't say the Feather Bed Mountains, sure that's the country like it is at the Red Cow, Blanchardstown and Lucan. The bog, brown butter, the poets call it, well I wouldn't like to be spreading it on me bread. But sure, even the Maggie Ryan that we did spread on our bread, it's called 'Summer Country Freshness'.

You see yeh can't get away from the country. The bog is cut wet and left to dry in the golden sun where it grows old and hairy like Oisin when he fell from his horse in Tír na nÓg (Land of Youth), which everyone knows is in the country down by Cork and not in Dublin. The turf is then taken by a red-headed boy and a donkey to the little white cottage on the green hillside to be cremated into white ashes that never go out and keep on burning like the Olympic flame in Athens. White ashes for the purity of the country soil, and we in Dublin with the grey greasy dirty setts, cobblestones and tarmacadam motorways, juggernaut fumes and oily buses. The hidden Ireland, Celtic romances, Celtic twilight, the Book of Kells, the Cross of Cong, the Ardagh Chalice, the Tara Brooch, they are all from the country and there's millions more. Paddy Kavanagh spent twelve months in Dublin looking for one lousy word for to finish a poem. Oh' Maud Gonne MacBride I love the memory of your name, I love the memory of your life and I love your cause, but why did you have to see Cathleen Ní Houlihan, the Queen of Ireland, coming across the bog in County Mayo? Why didn't you see her running down Stoneybatter or Francis Street? It would have given the Dublin poets and writers wonderful inspiration.

12

Ha'penny Cigarette and a Match

THE OLD BLACK MAGIC of a ha'penny Woodbine and a match was hard to beat in my childhood. Sometimes, we didn't need the match, just the Woodbine. 'Just give us the Woodbine, Mister, ya can keep the matches.'

In summertime all our Woodbines were lit by the golden sun and magnifying glasses, or some specky kid donated his specs to do the job. Small magnifying glasses were used for looking at insects, worms, chandlers, flies, bluebottles and lighting cigarettes. There was always a sense of achievement as we watched the sunlight mingle with the tobacco and bore a small black pin-point hole in it. Within seconds the black hole spread across the cigarette changing its colours into red and grey, and sending up a stream of blue smoke. A steady hand gave a good light with an even red glow across the top of the cigarette. A shaky hand gave a poor light and the cigarette lit down the side. In such cases, we wet the cigarette with our tongues under the side light and this method gave an even red glow. Side lights on cigarettes meant that we were in love. 'Oh! look at the way it lit, you're in love.' For a moment or two the cigarette was forgotten as we looked at the girls playing piggy beds and skipping, and wondered about love. Our romantic dreams were suddenly shattered when some kid would shout out 'Butts on ya Mack?'

I was nine years old, the early coughing fits and splutters and green faces were well gone, and my fingers bore the

There's Wagon Wheels,
There's Under the Arch,
There's In the Shade of an Old Apple Tree
And there's Danny Boy.
Hey! Mack, Where's Danny Boy?

95

brown nicotine stains. On my way to school each morning I rubbed my hands on the granite wall at Finerty's shop and entered my class with brand new thumb and finger tops. At lunch-hour break football conversation was mixed with questions. 'Hey Mack, any fags, any weeds, any butts, any stabbers, any coffin nails?'

Secret arrangements were made to meet down the lane after school for smokes, butts and a few drags. All smoking was done in secret. But some old wan always caught us. 'I'll tell yer mother I saw you smoking dirty butts and stabbers'.

The mother was always waiting with the leather belt. I was ate, bate and threw up again, but still I smoked. The hiding was one thing, but the grave warning never ended. 'You'll die. Yeh won't grow. Yer hair will fall out. Yer teeth will go black . . . You'll set fire to yourself.' To stop us smoking I think they would have had to shoot us. Maybe it was because they were strictly forbidden to children and only for grown ups, or maybe it was to dare the grave warnings. While there might be a toss up between gur cake and bullseyes, there was never a toss up when it came to smokes. Whenever we got a ha'penny, we ran down to the nearest shop. 'A ha'penny cigarette and a match, Mister . . . A ha'penny cigarette and a match, Missus.'

The shops had a Jacob's biscuit-tin lid with loose Woodbine cigarettes stacked like the pyramids of Egypt. Along the side of the tin lid were little heaps of red top matches. We always got two or three matches to enable us to nip the cigarettes and keep the big butt for the big picture or for later. Sometimes four of us would bunch in a ha'penny each and buy a packet of five Woodbines for tu'pence. Then we held a raffle or played a card game of 'Twenty-Five' or 'Rummy' to see who got the extra cigarette. The big fellas on the corner all bought packets. The brands they smoked were Woodbines, Kerry Blue, Tento, Drumhead, Players Weights, Picadilly, Clubs and Park Drive. Woodbines were always the poor man's smoke. Other men smoked Players, Afton, Marino, Craven A, Gold Flake, Gallaghers Blues, Richmond

Gem, and Capstan. The aristocrats of cigarettes were Churchman and Passing Cloud. We used to think that Churchman were for priests, bishops and Proddy Woddy ministers. Three Nuns Tobacco was supposed to be for convents, but we knew that was a joke. We could never imagine the Rev. Mother in Goldenbridge and Basin Lane sucking a white clay pipe and blowing smoke rings. Tara Street Railway Station had a cigarette machine and for a penny, and later tu'pence, we got a Churchman cigarette packed in a box. We were really millionaires then. Passing Cloud were oval shaped or like as if someone had sat on them.

Once a month Will's van dumped the broken and crushed cigarettes on the tip-head beyond Suir Bridge. It was a poor day's picking if we didn't get twenty Passing Cloud cigarettes and dozens of half Gold Flake and Woodbines. Any plug and shag tobacco collected was given to the old men who sat outside the old men's home in Kilmainham. These men were out of the Old Soldiers' Home.

Old Soldiers never die, they only fade away.
All Soldiers love the leg of a duck,
All Soldiers never get half enough,
Old Soldiers never die, they only fade away.

The old soldiers used to say, 'Sit beside me, don't annoy me, play with the chain of my watch'.

They never took the tobacco for nothing, it was an exchange transaction. Pennies, sweets, soldiers' buttons, soldiers' badges and safety pins. They spent their days between the home, the seat, and the Welcome Inn public house. They dozed on the seats but as soon as we arrived with the tobacco they were all wide awake, filling their clay pipes and puffing like blazes. One old soldier had no pipe but he still put out his hand for his share. We watched him as he chewed the tobacco and let out tobacco spits which landed in the middle of the road.

There was great competition between cigarette manufacturers, and advertising was everywhere. The 'David Allen' bill boards gave the different stories. The sportsman smoked Marino cigarettes because they were packed in waterproof and non-crush packets. There was a picture of a fisherman up to his eyeballs in a river, smiling because his Marino were waterproof. The Afton man got free coupons and free dinner sets. But later the Afton man had to pay an extra penny or tu'pence for his coupons and then coupons disappeared. The Gold Flake lady got small playing cards which could be exchanged for packs of big playing cards or other gifts. Players and Gallaghers gave free cigarette pictures, which could also be exchanged for gifts. 'Mister, any cigarette pitchers? . . . Mister, any little playing cards?'

We never asked for coupons, after all they had to pay extra for the coupons, but cards and cigarette pictures were for nothing. Cigarette pictures were like little universities, we learned everything from them and collected them by the hundred. We knew every jockey in the flat and hurdle races. We knew every bird, fish, footballer, church, cathedral and the Seven Wonders of the World. Cigarette pictures were nearly as good as the 'Fourpenny Rush' for learning and education. We studied them, played cards with them, swopped them, and sold them at eighty for a penny. Kerry Blue cigarettes gave a half coupon on the lid of the packet of five and a whole coupon on the packet of ten. These coupons could be exchanged for the following gifts:

> Alarm Clock — 250 coupons
> Box Camera — 230 coupons
> Pair Gents boots, black or brown — 750 coupons
> Pocket Watch — 260 coupons
> Tweed Cap — 125 coupons
> Art Silk Tie — 260 coupons
> Hair Clippers — 130 coupons
> (please state if the clippers is for fine or coarse hair)

Craven A cigarettes were made specially to prevent sore throats and the David Allen bill boards had a picture of an opera singer having a few drags before going on stage to sing his final aria.

As well as smoking Woodbines, butts and stabbers, we made badges out of the cigarette packets — drums and drum sticks, sailors' black cats, Kerry Blue dogs. We made boats out of the other packets and held boat races on the Camac River. Bobby Burns, the poet, 'Flow gently, Sweet Afton', nearly won every race. The Marino waterproof packets always sank. The silver paper was given to the nuns to save black babies, the gelatine was used for covering the picture in our magic shoe boxes. We told stories with the five Woodbine packet.

'There's Wagon Wheels, there's Under the Arch, there's In the Shade of an old Apple Tree, and there's Danny Boy.' Now the kids could see the Wagon Wheels, the Arch and the Apple Tree, but they couldn't see Danny Boy.

'Hey! Mack, where's Danny Boy?'

'He's Under the Arch having a piss.'

Sailors home on leave always smoked French or Black Russian cigarettes. To get one of these, we were millionaires. They were ten times stronger than Woodbines. No wonder we never grew, no wonder our hair fell out, no wonder we lost our teeth, we'd have been dead only for the war. 'Sorry, no cigarettes.' We used to kick the shop counters and say, 'That shook them'.

We had to fall back on the old 'channel' flake. Do you remember the gent who used to walk down Grafton Street with a pin sticking out of the end of his umbrella and he picking up the Channel Flake and cigar butts. Then came the Yankie sailors with Camel, Yanks and Lucky Strike cigarettes, and sticks of chewing gum.

Any Gum, chum?
Any Càmels, Mack?

When the war ended the cigarette case and lighter became all the fashion. The lighter could light as many cigarettes as were available for lights. The match could only light two cigarettes, no one would take the third light off a match. It was a war story. The German soldier saw the first light, aimed at the second light and shot dead the third light.

Cigarette cases came in all shapes, sizes and design. The real class case was the one Woolworths sold for one shilling and ninepence. It was gold plated, with the initial of your christian name in a circle. Lighters have come a long way from the old cotton wool, wick, flint and double tin cases. A home-made tinder box with charcoal flint and razor blade was just as good as any swanky lighter. Gramophone needle boxes were dingers for tinder boxes, charcoal was made by burning the tail of an old shirt. The flint scraped with the razor blade onto the charcoal was a quicker light than the sun and the magnifying glass.

In the cowboy pictures at the Fourpenny Rush an Indian statue stood outside the tobacco shops. The sign of the Indian was the sign of smokes, maybe his name was 'Passing Cloud'. But the cowboys never smoked, it was always the head crook who smoked long cigars. Now in the old days in Dublin, long, long ago, the tobacco shops had statues of black kings outside the door. The Americans had Indians but we had kings. The only king to survive in Dublin lost his throne and royal title and became 'The Black Man Byrne of Patrick Street'. Not only did he lose his throne and title, but he nearly lost his head in the explosion at Robert Emmet's depot in 1803. I feel sorry for him now. His royal highness 'The Black Man Byrne' is living in the Civic Museum in South William Street and beside him on the wall is a no smoking sign.

It's easy known that Joe Rathbone is dead. Joe had a cigar divan and ventilated smoking lounge at 25 Upper Baggot Street. He boasted that he was well acquainted with all the comforts liable to crop up while his patrons were under the influence of the fragrant weed. He sold Judge Tobacco at seven shillings a pound, Military Tobacco at five shillings a pound, Honey Dew Tobacco sold to ladies at six shillings a pound. Maybe the Rev. Mother had her drag as well as the rest of us.

The first shop in Dublin to put its name over the door in

the Irish language was Cathal Mac Garvey's tobacco shop, 'An Stad' in North Frederick Street. He was fined five shillings for breaking the law by having his name in Gaelic over his shop. But the name 'An Stad' remained. In my teenage days we used to hold a ceilidhe dance every Saturday in the basement of 'An Stad'. Sometimes Brendan Behan came to give us a song. Brendan sang with his eyes closed. During the song we used to creep out of the room and when Brendan finished the song, the room was always empty. 'Dirty lousers' was the mild part of the litany before Brendan left. I think Brendan used to enjoy our game because he kept coming back to sing for us and we kept up the creep out.

Did you know that tobacco was grown in Ireland in seven centres in the year 1904: Louth, Meath, Offaly, Kilkenny, Wexford, Cork and Limerick. The best tobacco farm in the country was at Randalstown, County Meath. They say 'Give every man his Dew', and so I will. Messrs. T. P. and R. Goodbody opened a factory in Tullamore, County Offaly, in the year 1843 to manufacture tobacco. Their first brand was Irish Roll, which gave its name to the saying, 'the heart of the rowl'. The centre of the Irish Roll tobacco was the freshest and juiciest. It was hand-made from start to finish. The manufacture of Primrose cigarettes was commenced in 1882. This cigarette appears to be the first cigarette manufactured in Ireland. It too was hand-made and hand-rolled by two hundred and twenty girls and one hundred men, and it was the popular brand until the advent of the machine-made thru'penny packet. In 1886 the factory transferred to Dublin after a fire and became known as the Greenville Tobacco Factory. Goodbodys were famous for tobacco, cigarettes and snuff. I worked one time in the basement of the Custom House, emptying snuff bags, but I never took a pinch. I didn't have to: I was paid three shillings by Carrolls for every snuff bag I emptied. It was tough work on me and my nose.

The next time you go down by Parliament Street, turn into Essex Gate and look up at the big building on your right hand side. At the top of the building you will see the lettering 'L. F. founded 1780'. This was Lundy Foot's Tobacco

Factory. Lundy's grave is in Irishtown Churchyard. He had two famous brands of pipe tobacco, High Toast and Irish Blackguard. Both of these were household names in China, India and Japan. Put that in your pipe and smoke it.

103

13

The Chief Bottle Washer

SINCE TIME IMMEMORIAL Dubliners have been nick-naming people, places and events. Nothing is too sacred or too holy to escape the nickname.

In slang the priest is the *sky pilot,* and the convent is the *prayer factory.* The *Domine, Christus, Sanctus,* in the old Latin Mass were nicknamed into *Dominick Street, Patrick Street, Christchurch* and the *Coombe.* The Oblate Fathers were one time known as the *Body Snatchers* and the Redemptorists were known as the *Boys that put the wind up yeh.* Father Kavanagh, who said the one o'clock 'Drunkards' Mass in High Street Chapel, was known as *Flash.* He could say the old Latin Mass in ten minutes flat. I think the earliest religious nickname was the one given to St. Mobhi of Glasnevin. He was called *Clarineach,* or in English, *Flat Face.*

Strongbow was the nickname of Richard Fitzgilbert. Dean Swift was a terrible man for handing out nicknames. To him, nearly everyone was a yahoo or a mope. He also gave three ladies nicknames, Jane Waring became *Varina,* Hester Johnson became *Stella* and Esther Vanhomrigh became *Vanessa.* He also called her a *slut* and her drawing-room the *sluttery.*

Some people show their affection by jeering and nick-naming other people. Some nicknames are given in wit, yet others are given in cruelty. Lord Clonmel was known as *Copper Face Jack,* Lord Norbury, the hanging judge, was

Sticks and stones
Will break my bones,
But names will never hurt me.
You called me this,
You called me that,
You called me a big fat pussy cat.

105

called *Bladder Chops*. The face seemed to be the first part of the body to become the subject for nicknames. I've known a few *Funeral* faces, *Moonbeam* faces, *Pontius Pilate* faces and faces that would *stop a clock*.

'What are you looking at?' 'Not much.' 'Well, look in the mirror and you will see less.'

The rest of the body was nicknamed as *baldy conscience, gunner eye, cauliflower ears, gummy, nosey parker, specky four eyes, mouth almighty*. 'There's only one mouth bigger than yours, it's *Portsmouth*.' 'That fellow would give an *Aspro a headache*.' Then there was *Knocker Knees, Footy*, and *Here's Me Head, Me Arse is coming* or *Open Your Legs, Here's a Barrel*.

Tiny was a seven foot policeman who stood at Westmoreland Street watching for bikes with no lamps or brakes. *Sampson* was a small, thin, meek man who worked on the Dublin docks. *Show Your Teeth* prayed in Whitefriar Street Chapel. There are dozens of *Head the Ball, Buckets, Barreller, Shoveller, Whacker, Porky, Fatso, Skinny, The Boss, Gaffer, Head Buck Cat* and *The Chief Bottle Washer*, all of them wore white coats, which gave the meaning to the saying *'The place is black with white coats'*. Policemen, among other things, were known as *Bobbies, Peelers, Poliss, Cops, Rawsers*, and *The Law*. Of course every cop on the beat had his own nickname. *Mandrake* was so called because his cloak used to fly in the wind as he made chase on his old-fashioned upstairs model of a B.S.A. bike. B.S.A. stood for Birmingham Small Arms, but again it was nicknamed into *Bloody Sore Arse*. I've known cops by the name of *Lugs, Brasso, Red Neck, Flat Foot, Porter Belly, Tarpo, Gogo, Blue Bottle*, and a dozen other names I could not put into print.

In my childhood days, very few uniform cops could run fast, so you can imagine the scene at any street corner waiting for the local bobby. No matter what his name was, he was called every nickname that came into our heads. When the 'Chase' began, the bobby was left hay-making.

Policeman, Policeman, don't take me,
I have a wife and a family,
How many children have you got?
Twenty-four, that's the lot.

In the first half of this century there were at least three hundred stone workers around Barnacullia. Doyle was the most common name, so it was essential to have a nickname. So here's to the Doyles that went by the following nicknames: *The Flier, The Hearse Man, Luby, Daddy, Lack, Rubbish, Dresser, Drummer, Gigger, Gulliver, Fecker, Softener, Tosser.* Other stone-cutting nicknames worthy of mention are *Gem, Feck, Weasel, Brewer, Peddlar, Crock, Mouldy, Urchin, Bantie, Snuggie, Sirle. Guncher* was considered to be the best stone cutter in Ireland.

Every school and workplace has its lore of nicknames. The docks and the coalyards gave forth *Horsey* by the score. There was *Heno, Bubbles, Whacko, Rats, Mousey, Kittens, Lulu, Granny, Brush,* who used to clean the gutter with one foot as he walked along Guild Street, and *Minute,* who always said 'wait a minute'. I remember seeing a group of dockers standing at the corner of Macken Street; as another group of dockers passed, the first group began to sing:

Here's the robbers passing by, passing by, passing by,
Here's the robbers passing by, my fair lady.

The group passing by turned and sang:

What did the robbers do to you, do to you, do to you.
What did the robbers do to you, my fair lady.

And they replied:

Stole my watch and stole my chain
In Bow Lane, in Bow Lane.
Stole my watch and stole my chain, my fair lady.

107

I worked with a fellow one time and his uncle was the *Boss.* So the fella was known in the office as *The Man from Uncle.* I with my hearing aid have been described by kids as the man with the *bionic ear.* There is no end to the nicknames and the Dublin wit is only waiting to show his skill.

Now I don't think that the *Toucher Doyle* was any relation to the noble stone workers of Glencullen and Barnacullia. Be that as it may, the *Toucher Doyle* left his mark on the ancient city of Dublin. Among the great stories of his great touching (borrowing) deeds, the best one is about the day he touched the Prince of Wales for the loan of five shillings and got it. The Prince was on a tour of Dublin's slumland in mufti. At first the people thought he was a landlord, but Charles Cameron, who was with him, told the people he was the Prince of Wales. That was enough for the *Toucher Doyle,* he was in like a shot and out again five shillings richer. I've known many touchers in my day and their name wasn't Doyle. The *Toucher Doyle* has been dead for many a year now but his noble trade goes on in the streets and pubs of Dublin.

If any one called a girl or a woman a bitch, she usually answered by saying 'A bitch is a dog, a decent dog, but you yeh pup, yer nothing'. The *Tuggers* was the nickname for the women who collected old clothes in big wicker boxcars and gave out cups and saucers. The *Rooney Pickers* are those who pick cinders, bottles, jam jars, and scrap metal on the dumps of Dublin.

Nearly every area has its own special nickname; *The Pocket* in Temple Street, *Dedra* for Drumcondra, *The Bower* in Sundrive Road, *The Temple* at Broadstone, *Norrier* for North Circular Road, *Nal* for the Canal, *Feeno* for the Phoenix Park. *The Puck, The Ranch, The Hole in the Wall, The Barn, Little Italy, Gibralta, Little Jerusalem* and the *Four Corners of Hell* beyond St. Patrick's Cathedral, also *Thomo, Jambo, Franner, Synger, Brunner, Tivo, Mayro, Feeno, Roto,* the last four referring to picture houses.

The letters O and R are made great use of in nicknames: *Flano, Redser, Byrner, Micko, Jacko, Dano,* and a million more. Wellington Street was *Old Wellier* and Pat O'Brien was known in the Fruit and Vegetable Market as the *Duke of Wellington*. Pat was a decent man and his small shop was the local supermarket of his day. Pat sold everything from bread, Maggie Ryan, butter, paraffin oil, loose jam, coal, candles and pot herbs. Tupence worth of pot herbs consisted of a turnip, onion, fistfull of parsley, thyme, celery and four scallions. Other nicknames around the neighbourhood were the *Sheriff Woman, Doleful Deirdre, Gorilla Woman, Huffy, Snuff, Gypsie Bill, Killybegs Joe, Cocker Boss* and the king of them all, *Willow,* who sunk the *Titanic. Willow,* poor old *Willow,* he was blamed for everything. 'Who took Napoleon off St. Helena? *'Willow.'* 'Who shot the Tsar of Russia?' *'Willow,'* and *Willow* protesting that he never met the Tsar or Napoleon in his life. A little old lady was *Willow's* champion. She would say, 'Ah for God's sake, can't yis let bygones be bygones.'

109

14

Vote Early and Often

A WELL-KNOWN LADY told me once that she voted seventeen times in the 1918 general election. When she was going back to the polling station for her thirteenth vote, the R.I.C. constable on duty at the door called her over. 'Excuse me, madam,' he said, 'but if you are thinking of coming back for another few votes, will you please change your fox fur collar as it's a dead give away.'

Vote early and often, even the dead in Glasnevin and Mount Jerome come out in their dozens at every election to exercise their franchise. It all starts on the canvas marking up the register. 'Ah! he's dead, but you can use his vote, he was always one of yours, voted for yis even when yis lost yer seat.' . . . 'Hold on a minute and I'll see if his voting card has arrived. The dead, the sick, the emigrants, the people that would not be able to make it to the polling station, all were willing to allow their votes to be used freely for the party. On the canvass everyone was voting for the party, at least that was what they said to get the door shut. If the elections were decided on the canvass, every party would have a majority. The only trouble was that as kids, we didn't stay with the same party from election to election. We switched around a bit. There were two main factors in helping us to decide who we'd canvass with. The first factor was ginger beer and doughnuts. The second factor was good-looking candidates. 'Janey, I'm not canvassing for that baldy looking

Vote, vote, vote for de Valera,
In comes Cosgrave at the door,
De Valera is the one
Who will have a bit of fun
And we don't want Cosgrave any more.

old fella.'

As the build up to the election got under way, the monster rallies were all held at the Black Lion in Inchicore. Each party sent its big guns. Dev, for Fianna Fáil, Dillon for Fine Gael and Norton for Labour. All the rallies had torchlight processions and we marched in every one of them. The meetings were great gas, hecklers by the dozen and several digging matches. The chairman introducing Dev got carried away with his own words: 'Dev,' he said, 'who worked for yis, fought for yis and even died for yis,' and Dev sitting behind him on the platform. Dev wasn't a great speaker, but the big crowd were listening in silence. Then the hecklers started. 'Who caused the Civil War?' This was the bell for round one. 'Who caused the Civil War?' The fists were flying now in all directions, we never knew who caused the Civil War but we did know that if the digging broke up the meeting, we got no ginger beer and doughnuts. Sometimes the fights were powerful, so to egg it on a bit, we'd road, 'Who caused the Civil War?'

Dillon was a great man for the hecklers. Some said that he paid the hecklers so that he could answer back and make fun of them in front of the crowd. Well, we believed this until the night the little ould fella kept shouting, 'Who took the shilling off the old age pensioners?' There was only blue bloody murder and no doughnuts.

The character candidates for us in childhood days were Alfie Byrne and Peadar Doyle. Alfie wasn't in our area but we were all plugging for him. He was a great man for the kids and the poor. He was the Lord Mayor and had been elected dozens of times. His pastime was shaking hands with people. When old Henry Ford came to Dublin, he said to Alfie, ' Who are you, sir?'

'I'm the man that shook hands with half of Ireland,' said Alfie.

'Well,' said Ford, 'I'm the man that shook the other half with my Model T motor cars.'

Peadar Doyle was our local man. He lived on Tirconnell Road. His brother was killed by the Black and Tans. Peadar was a fitter in the Inchicore Railway Works before going full time as a politician and Lord Mayor of Dublin. He was Fine Gael and he didn't get the mother's vote. He was highly respected as a man of integrity. When he was Lord Mayor, he was walking down the road one day, and an old woman stopped him. 'Oh! Mister Lord Mayor Doyle, will ya get me two sons jobs?' 'I will in me hat,' said Peadar, 'I can't get a job for me own son.'

So much for jobs for the boys and the girls as we see happening today. Peadar gave two great big candleabra to St. Michael's Church in memory of his late wife. The candles were never lit on it. We waited for years to see them lighting but they never saw a match not even when Peadar was elected to the Dáil. Then Peadar got married for a second time and we all said the candles will never be lit now. We were nearly going to send a deputation to the parish priest to demand the lighting of Peadar's candles.

Now and again, the clergy took an interest in the elections. Under pain of mortal sin we weren't to vote for the Communist, whose election slogan was 'A Swimming Pool for the Kids'. All we said was, 'They won't light the candles and they don't want us to swim.' The Commie got seventy-six votes and everyone said that the P.P. was out every night looking for the seventy-six mortal sinners. Oh! the Commies were coming alright. The next thing was the Co-op — a small shop on the back road selling groceries far cheaper than any shop in Dublin. The Russians owned it. The Co-op was a cover for the Reds. 'Don't go near the Co-op, it's controlled from Moscow.' The Co-op was about the size of a postage stamp. We were standing looking into the Co-op window one day; there was six tins of Casserole stew, a few boxes of Fry's Cocoa and about two dozen packets of Lot's Wife salt. The salt packets were blue and white in colour with a picture of Lot's wife looking back and turning into a pillar of salt. 'I think the P.P. was right,' said me pal, 'that's Russian salt.'

Oh! the Reds were coming all right. This was their third attempt to invade Ireland. Reds under the bed, Reds in the City Hall and Reds trying to get into Leinster House. Russian gold, the Spanish Civil War and even the big R.O.P. oil tankers were Russian Oil Products and the tankers were all driven by K.G.B. agents. Russian ships and sailors were all watched with caution. Even our favourite film stars and cowboy heroes were all Reds in disguise. 'Red Stars over Hollywood', 'Red Stars over City Hall', 'Red Stars over Leinster House', and to make matters worse the Black Russian cigarettes were everywhere. Hammers and sickles, Black Russian cigarettes, R.O.P. oil tankers and funny-looking ould fellas wearing fur hats like the ones they wore in Moscow. The hotels were full of Commies. Commie waiters, Commie chefs. We even had a local red living near us who never went to Mass on a Sunday. The anti-Communist League went into action to see that there was no 'vote early and often' for the Reds. We couldn't even queue up for the pictures in peace. We were told by the League members that our ninepences were going to Moscow and that we should boycott the Red film stars and the Reds in general. 'Red Stars over Hollywood', they shouted out as the queue moved forward to the cash box. We couldn't keep our minds on the picture. It was hard to imagine the Durango Kid's ould fella was a Red. He didn't even wear a fur hat. Despite the Reds, the elections went on.

The Corpo' elections were never as good as the general elections. Some of the Corpo' ones were damp squibs. It was a different ball game with not as many motor cars, rallies, ginger beer or doughnuts. Not as many people came out to vote and there was hardly ever a fight at the Black Lion. One policeman did duty at the Corpo' elections, it took six or sometimes ten policemen to do duty at the general elections. Whenever a fight broke out it was one up in social status to be taken by six policemen. Dano's ould fella was powerful, it took six cops to hold him down. Jimmy's ould fella wasn't a good scrapper, four cops could take him.

I knew a man whose brother was going up for a Dáil seat. 'How will the brother do?' I asked. 'Well, it's like this,' he said. 'There's fifty-one in our family, and if my brother only gets fifty votes he'll kick up such a row to find out who didn't vote for him that it will take six cops to quieten him down.'

'How's the election going?' I asked another candidate. 'Powerful,' he said. 'I've been to two funerals today and I'm going to a wedding tomorrow.'

15

Scut the Whip

I NEVER SAW a horse being bought and sold for one and nine in old money, which as everyone knows is thru'pence less than two bob, or in today's value a ten pence piece. Isn't it funny how two bob which was always twenty-four old pence is now only ten? And could you imagine being sent out by your mother to buy a horse and told to keep the thru'pence change for bullseyes?

The cheapest horse I ever saw wasn't sold, he was gambled on 'harps' at the pitch-and-toss school in the Brickfields for ten pounds. 'Go wan now, sir,' said yer man, 'I've the flyers on the feck. Put your horse where your mouth is. I'll lay ten quid to that bag of bones and the cab that I'll head them.' The other man looked at his horse and cab, looked at the crowd who egged him on and looked back at yer man with the flyers. Flyers were two black Victorian ha'pennies which were gold polished from the Brickfield sands. The feck was one half of an old blue-coloured comb. The horse didn't look too interested in who would be his master as he ate his supper from the green weeds growing out of the side of the Rock Mountain. The Rock Mountain was made of rock, so the horse was lucky for it was the only bit of green in sight. The swift flowing mill race stood between the horse and the green banks of the Grand Canal. Up went the flyers — a head and a harp. Up went the flyers again — another head and a harp. The suspense was beginning to tell on the toss man, the

116

Johnston Mooney and O'Brien,
Bought a horse for one and nine.
When the horse began to kick,
Johnston Mooney bought a stick.
When the stick began to wear
Johnston Mooney began to swear.
When the swear began to sell,
Johnston Mooney went to Hell.

air was electric. Up went the flyers for the third time. Down they came twirling and up looked Victoria's two heads. The crowd was silent as the toss man picked up his ten pound note and took the whip out of the horseman's pocket. Then the roar went up in waves along the canal. The toss man examined his prize in detail. He looked at the horse's teeth first. 'They're very bloody black,' said he, 'how old did you say he was?' The horseman mumbled something, pushed through the crowd and was gone in a flash. 'He looks ould,' said the tossman, 'and he could sure do with the belt of a currycomb.' Yesterday's dinner was still on the horse's hind legs. 'The cab could do with a coat of paint,' said the tossman, 'and the back wheel is buckled but it won't take much to fix it. Hey, Barreller,' he called to another man, 'di ya think will he be able to draw a load of wash?' Before Barreller could answer another man shouted to the tossman, 'He's only fit for O'Keefe's the Knackers.'

The first horse that I ever saw as a child, or at least the first horse that I can remember, wasn't a horse at all. It was a ginnett. But to me at five years of age it was the nicest horse in Dublin. It hadn't any name of its own. It was known far and wide in the Liberties, Kilmainham and Inchicore as Ennis's ginnett. Mr. Ennis who collected the slop (pig feeding) always called the horse the ginnett. 'Will ya keep an eye on the ginnett, son. Don't go near the ginnett's head. If she starts to move just say "easy ginnett, easy ginnett".' She kicked like hell. She snapped her teeth at every bike that went by. She could do seven kick-ups with her hind legs all in one go. She could walk better backwards and sidewards than forward. The ginnett was the fear of me early childhood, but I loved every red hair in her body. The ginnett always brought an air of excitement to Kickham Road corner. She worked seven days a week at slop collecting, coal deliveries, orange selling and pony rides at Sandymount Strand on a Sunday and bank holidays. I saw the ginnett a few times at Sandymount Strand and she always looked as quiet as a mouse. The waiting on the slop didn't have the same peaceful effect on her as the salt sea air. 'Easy ginnett, easy ginnett,' as the slop barrell danced all around the cart keeping in step with the ginnett's hind legs.

One day the ginnett kicked so hard that she turned the barrell and its contents over. The smell was worse than O'Keefe's the Knackers but the ginnett didn't wait too long in the smell. She got the steel bit between her teeth and went up Goldenbridge Avenue like a racehorse. 'Runaway, mister, runaway, stop the runaway, mister,' as we charged up the Avenue after the ginnett. A few men made an attempt to stop the ginnett but quickly pulled away as they saw the ginnett's wild eyes coming at them. Then out of the blue came a small, thin man. We could see him in front of the ginnett. 'She'll ate him, she'll kill him,' everyone cried. Yer man just stood there, grabbed at the loose reins that were hanging down the side of the cart and pulled sideways. The ginnett lost the grip on the bit and ended up around the letterbox at Southern Cross Avenue. The hero, the small, thin man, hadn't a tooth in his head. He didn't look very strong but he was a wiry looking fella. 'Surprise, son, surprise, that's how it's done, it's all a matter of surprise,' said the small, thin man, glowing now, eyes shining, gummy mouth laughing as he drank in our hero-worship and shrugged his shoulders to our many pats on the back of his grey, worn, black overcoat. Mr. Ennis's face was as red as a tomato as he came up the Avenue panting with two buckets of slop. 'Oh me ginnett, oh me ginnett,' he kept saying. We wouldn't let the hero go. 'Mr. Ennis, this is the man that stopped the runaway ginnett.' Mr. Ennis thanked him and gave him a few bob and then examined the ginnett and the cart. We left Mr. Ennis and the ginnett and followed our hero down the Avenue, telling every passer-by, 'Mister, this is the man that stopped the runaway ginnett.' And the hero, going all shy, repeated the word, 'surprise, surprise'.

There was never a dull moment when the red ginnett came on the scene of our childhood. The runaway horse on the streets of Dublin was always like the wild west cowboy pictures when the stagecoach driver was shot by the crooks or the Indians and the six coach-horses became runaways. It was always one of my daylight dreams as a child that I would stop a runaway horse, but I never did. After all I knew the' trick, 'surprise, just surprise'. I've seen all sorts of runaway horses, I've even seen a runaway funeral horse flying down Mount Brown Hill. 'Runaway! Clear the road, stop the runaway, mister!' Well, Kerrigans never had any trouble with runaways. Kerrigans had an ass that had to be coaxed to walk. I think he was the only ass in Dublin that wouldn't eat grass.

> Kerrigan's ass
> Won't eat grass.
> Lift its tail
> And kick it
> In the arse.

Despite the lines of the verse we sang, I never saw anyone kicking or beating Kerrigan's ass, or any other horses for that matter. The horse, ass, ginnett, mule, were always treated with great love, respect and kindness. The beating of animals was always reserved for sheep and cows on their way to the cattle market on the North Circular Road. I think every kid in Dublin wanted to be a cattle drover or a shepherd.

A fair few of the canal barges were drawn by horses. It was a great pastime leading the horse along the Grand Canal banks from the first to the fifth lock. The journey with the horse was never tiring or dull, but the journey home on our own was brutal.

There were several places in Dublin where we used to love to play with the horses. Our first choice was always the Brickfields to see if we could catch and ride bareback the piebald ponies that belonged to the gypsies. The second choice was White's of Islandbridge, who had dozens of stables and trained horses. With a bit of luck the stablehand would allow us to feed the horses or hold the rope as the horse walked around in circles, but sometimes the gate would be locked and all we could do then was to sit on the wall with the old men and look down at all the horse action. The third choice was Coopers, Queen Street, watching the buying and selling of horses. But Coopers never allowed kids in the yard, so we had to try and slip in when the stableman wasn't looking. Coopers was easy enough to bunk into and sure if we were caught, all the stableman would do was roar at us, not like Islandbridge Barracks where we were nearly shot by the soldier sentry and all we wanted to do was look at a horse's grave. The army had lovely big horses and a lovely sight to see was a cannon gun drawn by a horse, with an artillery soldier sitting on the left shaft. The soldiers' barracks and the changing of the guard were always one of the main attractions, but the horse was king. At a certain time each day a group of horses came out of the soldiers' barracks drawing all sorts of carts and guns. Then someone told us that there was a horses' graveyard in Islandbridge Barracks. We tried to bunk into the barracks as the gates were opened to let out the horses. All we heard was the halt, then we saw the swinging gates of the Phoenix Park. I don't think I ran as fast in all me life. So we never got to see the horse's grave. I have since discovered, although I never have seen it, that there is a plaque in Islandbridge Barracks which reads: 'Under this spot lies buried the remains of Dickie Bird B7 Troop Horse Fifth Dragoon Guards which was foaled in 1850, joined the regiment in 1853 and served throughout the entire Crimean campaign from May 1854 – June 1856. He was shot on Nov. 21, 1874 by special authority from the Horse Guards to save him being sold by auction.' Wouldn't it have been a nicer tribute to have let poor ol' Dickie Bird ramble around Phoenix Park to the end of his days?

Whenever we saw a bony horse or a tired horse with his head bent down we always joked and jeered, 'Hey Mack, where are you taking your bag of bones to, O'Keefe's the Knackers?' Or if we saw a man whipping a horse up a hill, we always cried out, 'You're wasting your time mister, he's only fit for O'Keefe's the Knackers.' Do you know what I'm going to tell you, Mill Street will never be the same again since O'Keefe's the Knackers moved out. The smell was a great cure for Asian 'flu, and it made the Liffey smell seem like scented soap.

All the same didn't the ol' horse make a great contribution to the land of Ireland? Not just O'Keefe's celebrated manure but all the celebrated manure that was picked up by hand, shovel and buckets in every street in Dublin. A good bucket of manure was always worth fourpence or sixpence from a real green-fingered gardener. Horse manure got so plentiful that you could buy a cartload for five shillings delivered or you could draw it free yourself from the mountains of manure all over Dublin's stablehands. The horse was king. Give way to horse traffic and what a sight it was to see. The big post office van drawn by horses, the queue of those carts at Guinness Jetty, a line of Richardson's horses and Warham's horses, shires, clydesdales and Irish draught horses which we called hunters.

Bread vans, milk floats, coal drays, the B. & I., the L.M.S., all with their own style of horses. The trace horse helped the other horse to draw the cart up Cork Hill. The horsemen, each a character in his own right. 'Yup, yup, yup, hike, hike, hike', and the clip-clop of the horse's iron shoes on the cobblestone and setts.

The parade to the Royal Dublin Society Horse Show, with the black leather harness gleaming, studded with shining brass or silver haines, buckles, studs, bits of chain. The horseman sitting erect with bowler hat, spotless apron and shining black boots. The horse's tail plaited and red ribbon intertwined all along the hair of her neck. The Court and Mirror Laundry vans trotting along the Merrion Road on their way to collect their rosettes of blue and red ribbons and silver cups. The ovation in James's Street as the Guinness winners came home from Ballsbridge. And who remembers the Horseman Doyle? The pride of Warham's of Echlin Street who drew the grain, the hops and the malt for Guinness. The Horseman Doyle could carry two twenty-stone bags of grain under his oxters. He made a bet one night in a pub that he could carry the two twenty-stone bags from Watling Street to James's Street fountain. But the Horseman's wife found out about the bet and she told him that if he tried to win the bet she would up-end him in front of all his friends in the middle of James's Street. The wife must have really loved the Horseman Doyle. She was even prepared to up-end him to protect his health. Can you imagine the scene if the Horseman Doyle had went ahead with the bet? Here he is, coming up James's Street, and there's the wife, a big woman, nearly as big as the Horseman, sleeves rolled up, the shawl well tucked in around her neck and she waiting in his path to up-end him. I can nearly see the two bags of grain and the Horseman lying on the cobblestones. And the funny thing is I can see no one laughing.

'Scut the whip, mister, look behind, scut the whip.' The Horseman Doyle never paid heed to scut the whip warnings. A nod of his head, a shrug of his shoulders, but he never flicked the whip as we scutted his cart. Other horsemen flicked the whip at our hands and some got down to flick the whip at our arses, but the Horseman Doyle drove on, letting the scut take its natural course until we bade farewell and went to look for another scut home. 'Yup, yup, scut the whip, mister.' And may the light of Heaven shine on the Horseman Doyle and his missus, and on all the ol' horsemen of Dublin.

16

Walking Down O'Connell Street

FOR YEARS AND YEARS my half day was on a Saturday. I'd finish up work at one o'clock sharp and arrive home for my dinner at six o'clock in the evening. My mother was always mystified and the dinner looked the worse of the wear from waiting. The mother would look at me, look at the clock, then she'd say, 'What I can't understand is, how it takes a man five hours to get from the North Wall to Inchicore, what in the name of God were you doing?' My answer was always the same, 'I was walking down O'Connell Street.'

'Five hours' the mother would say. 'Five hours to walk down O'Connell Street, I'd do it in less than ten minutes'. What the poor mother didn't know was that my walking down O'Connell Street was something special. It started at the corner of Hopkins and Hopkins, but I suppose I should mention that I never started my walking 'till half past two. It took me a half hour to get from the North Wall to O'Connell Bridge, the other hour was always spent at Joe Clark's book barrow, on Eden Quay.

'Here's Joe now,' someone would say. Joe Clark, the Dublin street bookseller, came puffing and panting between the shafts of the green handcart laden with a mountain of books under sacking and rope. As soon as the rope and sacking was released, an avalanche of books started, yet I never saw a book touch the ground.

Amen means so be it,
Half a loaf and a thru'penny bit.
Two men, four feet,
Walking down O'Connell Street,
Shouting out pig's feet
One and four a pound.

Sixty hands, thirty chests and ten or twelve bellies held back the flood of knowledge. All hands on the handcart as sixty eyes quickly read the titles. The hands alone, told their own story. The woollen mittens of Professor Liam O'Broin, the coal-dust hands of the Dublin docker, the gold signet ring of the Doctor of Divinity from Trinity College stood out among the book collectors, just as noticeable as the broad black brimmer worn by Cathal O'Shannon. There's many a book on my shelf and there's many a scholar who got a little more knowledge from the books bought at Joe Clark's handcart.

Sometimes, the Professor and the Doctor of Divinity would gaze with me at the silverware in Hopkins and Hopkins' windows and sometimes I'd gaze alone. Hopkins and Hopkins changed the silver window display every week, the whole corner of O'Connell Street and Eden Quay was one mass of craftsmans' silver. It is no wonder the silversmiths gave us the word 'masterpiece'. The apprentice silversmiths had to spend seven years learning their trade. Then, to pass as a qualified silversmith he had to submit a piece of silver shaped and engraved to the master of the Goldsmiths and Silversmiths Trade Guild. This piece became known as the masterpiece. In my walking days, it was Jamesons for gold, McDowells for diamonds and Hopkins and Hopkins for silver. Having feasted my eyes on the beautiful silverware I would walk up to the Grand Central Cinema to see what picture was on and what were the forthcoming attractions, not that I ever went to the Grand Central, but just to see what sort of pictures were on their way to our locals. The Grand Central was an all-cushion cinema, no wooderners.

The Metropolitan Hall was all wooderners and no cushioners, it was sixpence in to see the Boys' Brigade drill displays and inspection parades. It was always a great show for a tanner with a real brass band, St. George's, playing all the marches and Wagner tunes. I was such a good customer at the Metropolitan Hall that the doorman let me in one Saturday for nothing. 'You don't have to pay, sir,' said he. On my way out he asked me if I was a member of All Saints,

Grangegorman? 'No,' I replied, 'I'm a member of St. Michael's, Inchicore, and the Oblate Sodality.' I didn't wait to hear what he said, nor did I look at the expression on his face. I was nearly afraid to go back now that I was caught on. I did go back and it was still free admission, and me and the doorman became great pals.

My next point of call was Clery's shop, the site of the old Imperial Hotel, where Jem Larkin addressed the crowd of strikers on Bloody Sunday 1913. Clery's was a swank shop, but then, our Mister Guiney took over in 1941, and although they didn't have the same green paper as Guiney's of Talbot Street, we were still customers and I visited the forty odd departments. Every shop window except one, got a quick look and some got a short study. The Fifty-Shilling Tailors, Gleeson's Boys Town, Kingston's, O'Beirne and O'Neill, later Fitzgibbon, got a study. I nearly ran past Madame Nora's, it was the only shop that I never looked at, it being strictly for women. Not even the delicious cream cakes in Kylemore's window could get me to slow my pace as I went down Cathedral Street and into Dermot Fitzpatrick's shop. Dermot was a great friend, he was a republican, a poet, scholar and an authority on the Treaty and the Spanish Civil War. The conversation usually started off with the weather and concluded with Frank Ryan and Spain. In half an hour I'd end up in the Pro-Cathedral, with four rows in front of me, for confession. An hour later I'd pay a visit to Moss Twoomey's shop at the corner of Cathal Brugha Street. Moss was another republican, a one-time Chief of Staff of the I.R.A. Sometimes he would talk and sometimes he would say nothing. I always took him as I found him, but many's the battle was re-fought in his sweet and cake shop. I never failed to give Parnell a salute as I crossed the street and went into Brian O'Higgins' shop. Brian was a 1916 man and the author of the *Wolfe Tone Annual.* He also wrote and published the great series of Irish Christmas cards. Brian was a real true-blood republican and everything he did was Irish to the backbone. Sometimes he'd say a few words but more times he'd say nothing. The lovely little Irish books he wrote went all around the world and it's true to say he kept the Irish ideal alive by his writings and publishing. I always spent a good ten minutes watching the blind men making baskets in the windows of the Richmond Institution, then it was a visit to the Pillar Picture Palace to see, again, the forthcoming attractions. The Pillar wasn't as posh as the Grand and looked a right flea house from the outside, but it always showed powerful pictures.

About this stage the hunger used to come on me, so I'd pay a quick visit to the Irish Book Bureau and have a chat with me old friend Joe Clarke, no, not the bookseller, another Joe Clarke, who fought at the battle of Mount Street Bridge in the 1916 Rising. Joe had a mountain of old republican newspapers, which he used to sell at a few pence each. After a few years I had the mountain of papers in my bedroom. Joe was a great character, the life and soul of Dublin wit and song. He could tell stories for a month without stopping. Dermot, Moss, Brian and Joe, I used to call them my four republican evangelists in O'Connell Street. I wouldn't even see Nelson's Pillar as I'd make a bee-line down to Freddy Hafner's shop in Henry Street. 'A quarter of cooked ham, please.' He had pigs' feet galore, but they weren't cooked. I used to get the ham cut up in little squares, so that it would be handy for eating out of my pocket. This day he was cutting the ham when a lady at the counter asked him why he was doing that? 'Oh, it's for Cocktail Cracker,' he said. 'That's nice,' said she, 'Will you do mine the same way?' There I was starting a new fashion in cut up cooked ham.

I always had a letter to post in the G.P.O. or maybe I'd buy a letter postcard for fourpence, a stamp for only tuppence, just imagine six letters for a shilling. I couldn't pass the Capitol or the Metropole Theatres without gazing and gazing. The Savoy and the Carlton got a quick look but the Capitol and the Met. got a study. Maybe it was the lovely Capitol girls showing their dancing legs in the showcases as well as the film stars. Or maybe it was the fancy toilets downstairs in the Met. and the sounds of Peggy Dell playing the piano that made me linger around Prince's Street corner. Next it was Eason's, downstairs and the secondhand books. Gilbert's *Calendar of Ancient Records of Dublin* for seventeen shillings and sixpence, and they had dozens of them. The *Life of Peg Woffington*, fifteen shillings, Collin's *Life in Old Dublin* for eighteen shillings and me with a pound pocket money for the week in me pocket. Oh! the bargains I had to pass up. I broke out one week and bought one of Gilbert's books, I still have it on my bookshelves, but I'll never forget the brutal week I had on my half dollar, and to make matters worse Dermot, Moss, Brian and the two Joe Clarkes asked me why I didn't call that week. After Eason's it was Mansfield's and Elvery's corner. Elvery's corner doesn't look the same since they removed the elephant from over the doorway. Lemon's Sweets and the Astor Cinema were the last two stops as I made my way around Bachelor's Walk to the Dublin Bookshop. The prices there were more in my line. Trays of books outside the shop and a penny bookstand in the doorway. Many's a penny gem I got. I think the dearest book outside in the street was a shilling. The popular stands were the penny, the fourpenny, and the sixpenny. Loaded as I was now with books, newspapers and magazines, all I had to do was to cross the street and get the 24 bus home, for me dinner and the Angelus bell.

17

Oh Gawney Mack! It's James Joyce

WELL, AT LEAST NOBODY can say that James Joyce didn't go out and hunt his own mot in his own way outside Kevin and Howlin's Tweed Shop in Patrick's Well Lane in 1904. He was having a bit of a dander along the footprints of St. Patrick wearing his sailor hat and looking like Captain Fish Fingers himself, when he spots this fine-looking, red-headed girl. Well, he gave her the 'glad eye' and the 'clicking' commenced. The mot was rushing back to Finn's Hotel, where she worked as a chambermaid. She ran one way thinking she had hooked a seafaring man, or maybe a man with his own ship or yacht out in Kingstown. He ran the other way up to Yeates' corner at Grafton Street to see his reflection in the highly polished windows and to see how he looked and if his sailor's cap was at the right angle. He was beaming like a Cheshire cat as he had a date with the lovely redhead for the next day, which was 14th June 1904.

Now, James Joyce, me old heart goes out to you. I know exactly how you felt when the redheaded mot didn't turn up. Sure it happened to us all, James. I meself was left standing outside the 'Met' in O'Connell Street and worse for me, I was after buying the Nutty Favourites. Now, I'm not sure whether James had the sweets bought beforehand or not. Faint heart never won fair lady, home James and don't spare the horses or the pen and paper. Well, that he didn't! He dropped a little letter into her hotel. Another date was fixed

One hundred years ago today,
When a wilderness was here,
The man with powder in his gun
Went forth to hunt the Deer.
But now, the times have changed
With quite a different plan,
The 'Dear' with powder on her nose
Goes forth to hunt the man.

2nd February 1882

for the corner of Merrion Square for the 16th June. They met outside Sir William Wilde's house, number 1 Merrion Square. He brought her for a walk to Ringsend and 'Bloomsday' was born.

The words 'Gawney Mack' is the swanky way of saying 'Janey Mack'. You see the word 'Gawney' suits the Rathgar accent, whereas the word 'Janey' would sound downright vulgar when used by people who speak pound notes. And as Mister James Joyce was born in Rathgar on the swanky side of Dublin, it's only fair and fitting to give him the swanky word of 'Gawney Mack'. He was born at 41 Brighton Square, Rathgar, Dublin, Ireland, Europe, The World, The Universe. James liked the full title of his address. But it wasn't really a square he was born in, it was a triangle. Now the swanks couldn't use the word triangle, it has too much of a Mountjoy Jail ring to it, so they called it Brighton Square. All the same now, the 'Old Triangle' is a lot sweeter on the ear than some of Joyce's Chamber Music.

For more years than I care to remember, I've been doing me own private 'Bloomsday' lark or thingamajig. Not just on the 16th June, like the literary jet set, scholars, professors, Yanks, horse cabs and barrel organs. No by Leopold Bloom's stuffed roast heart and liver slices, fried with breadcrumbs, I've been doing the Joycean act all my born days. Sure, wasn't I born in Rathmines Fire Brigade Station around the corner from Joyce's second home at 23 Castlewood Avenue? And amn't I on fire all my life with love for Ireland, Dublin, and Jemmy Joyce? The first time I saw Joyce's fourth home at 14 Fitzgibbon Street was the time I had bed and breakfast in Fitzgibbon Street Police Station. I ran with my laundry parcels all around Hardwicke Street, Millbourne Avenue, Windsor Avenue, Richmond Avenue, Royal Terrace, Inverness now North Richmond Street and St. Peter's Terrace. And I was driven in Switzer's charcoal juice motor van around Joyce's swanky houses, 1 Martello Terrace, Bray, Leoville, 23 Carysfort Avenue, Blackrock, and 35 and 103 Strand Road, Sandymount. I used to buy my suits at five shillings a week in the Volta Picture Palace in Mary Street. It was owned by Hipps then, and many's the time getting a fitting I could see Joyce with the silver flashlamp trying to quieten down the Tuppenny Rush! I worked for years around the corner from Joyce's eleventh house at Glengarriff Parade. Sure, that's where I used to park my secondhand bike that I bought from the cops in Kevin Street, and what's more I never had to use a lock and chain. Sean O'Casey's ghost kept an eye on it. In all, Joyce lived in eighteen houses in Dublin, not counting Buck Mulligan's tower in Sandycove or the places he slept in when he was out on 'Gur'. No wonder he wanted to be able to rebuild Dublin from his book *Ulysses.*

We went to Sandymount Strand, not just on 16th June, but every Sunday from May to September and we must have seen millions of Gerties. Now here is the daddy of it all! When I got married, the first place I lived in was 73 Eccles Street, nearly opposite Leopold Bloom's house at number 7. The first thing I saw every morning was 'Bloom' slipping out for his liver slices. Once, I was nearly going to ask him for the loan of a cup of sugar, but I didn't like his Missus. There was no loose coalhole cover outside our house. Not that we minded, we lived on the sixth floor and had to carry up the Lullymore briquettes one by one. On Sundays we went for a walk to the Basin in Blessington Street and home by Joyce's house in Fontenoy Street. We didn't use Lemon Soap but we drank Lemon drinks when we had the 'flu. We didn't read *Sweets of Sin,* but we read every penny horrible and dirty book you may care to mention.

And wasn't Blazes Boylan coming out of the Ormond Hotel as me and the Missus were going in for our wedding reception. Now all this goes to show that we're no Johnny-come-latelys. James Joyce Dubliners, and maybe this was the reason why James Joyce appeared to me instead of all the Joycean scholars. I'll tell you how it happened.

I was coming out of Fred Hanna's bookshop in Nassau Street, when I bumped into this fella wearing a sailor's cap. 'Excuse me,' said he, 'but did you see a redheaded girl in there?' 'No,' said I, 'the only redheaded girl I know is the one

133

Gogarty wanted to live with in Ringsend.''

'Don't mention that man's name,' said the sailor. 'Do you know who I am?'

'Well, now, the old face is familiar,' I said. 'Do you be on the telly?'

'Telly me arse,' said the sailor. 'I'm James Joyce, I've come home for my Centenary Birthday Celebrations. I hear that they are going to have great gas in Trinity College and that they are thinking of putting a statue of me on top of the Wellington Monument.'

'Shit and onions,' said I. 'Sure you wouldn't print that name, would you? You said so yourself in your lovely poem "Gas from a Burner".'

'Ah!' said he, 'I'm changing like Sean O'Casey did with the Abbey.'

'Well, says I, you needn't worry about Sydney Parade and the Sandymount tram. The trams are all gone for their tea.'

'I noticed that,' said Joyce. 'Monto gone as well and where's the O'Brien statue that was at the corner of D'Olier Street and did they put the Ballast Office clock on the side of the building at Aston's Quay to fool poor old Endymion?' Before I could answer, Joyce asked me for the loan of five shillings.

'Well, I'm not taking your photograph, but I'll give you a half a note if you show me the very spot where you and the redheaded girl Nora Barnacle met in Merrion Square.'

'What size boots do you take,' said he, 'and have you any spare shirts?'

'Show me the spot, James, where you and Barnacle Bill's daughter Nora met and I'll give you a quid and bring you to the Daisy and the Iveagh Markets and you can pick boots and shirts to your heart's content.'

'You're on,' said he, 'let's go.'

As we walked up Nassau Street he told me the Volta Picture House failed because he didn't show the 'Follyin-upper'. Well, he was a fast walker and he was swinging his cane stick goodo and he sniffed the fresh bread outside Johnston Mooney's (O'Brien's shop in Leinster Street). The only stop he made was outside Greene's bookshop, where he flicked through all the books on the outside stands. 'Come on inside,' said I. 'Upstairs in the Nookway is where they keep all the gems.'

'Fire away,' said he.

I took the stairs two at a time and had the Nookway all to myself. Sure didn't I get so caught up in all the gems of books that I nearly forgot about James Joyce. When I came down the stairs looking for him wasn't the shop crowded with youngwans and youngfellas buying school books. Not a sign of James anywhere. I looked and looked but he was gone like the canal water at Rialto 'Bridge. Then I began to think he must have gone up to Merrion Square corner and maybe he's waiting for me. He's not going to pass up a pound note, boots and shirts, said I to myself. Up I goes to the corner, not a sight or sound of him. I spotted an old lady sitting on the Rutland Fountain and I decided to ask her if she saw Mister James Joyce. 'Excuse me Mam, did you see James Joyce anywhere near the Rutland Fountain?'

'This is not the Rutland Fountain,' said she. 'This is my Fountain.'

'And who are you?' I asked.

'I'm Sybil Le Brocquy and my friends gave me this fountain. Look,' she said, 'read it for yourself.'

'There's no water,' said I.

'No,' said she, 'it's gone like your Mister Joyce. Go ask that man standing over there on the bit of a wall,' she said.

I crossed the street and saw the name Dargan written on the bit of a wall. 'Excuse me Mr. Dargan, did you see James Joyce the writer?'

'What do I know about writers,' he said, 'I'm a railwayman myself.'

'What's all this about Fastrack and Main Line Rail?' And who closed Harcourt Street Railway Station?' he said.

'Well Dublin made us, Mister Dargan, but I think you better ask Todd Andrews that question.'

'There's a writer behind me,' said Dargan, 'but I don't think his name is Joyce.'

135

' 'deed and it's not,' said the fellow behind. 'My name is George Bernard Shaw, go on in son and have a decko at my pictures in the Art Gallery.. Oh and by the way did they fix that window I broke in Whitefriar Street Chapel?' G.B.S. did all the talking; he wanted me to take him out to Dalkey Hill to pick 'blackers'. Well, I told him I hadn't the time and besides I was looking for Joyce. 'Maybe he's hiding behind me,' said Shaw. Right enough I did hear noises of some bushes moving, so I moved into the corner and there was another fellow standing up on a bit of a wall. He had his back to me so I called out, 'Is that you Jemmy Joyce?'

Your man turned around and started to cry. 'No,' said he, 'I'm Parke. I'm Surgeon Parke that saved Stanley's life the time we were looking for Livingston in the Jungle and here I am stuck in this little jungle and I can't find my way out. At one time I was out there in the front with a lovely view of the Rutland Fountain, but now that bloody tree is blocking me view.'

'The Sybil Le Brocquy Fountain,' I said.

'That's a nice name,' said Parke, 'sounds better than Rutland.'

'Ah,' said I, 'she was a lovely lady and I had the great honour to propose a vote of thanks to her in the Spa Hotel, Lucan on the day she gave the Old Dublin Society a talk on the history of Lucan.'

'I wish,' said Parke, 'someone would give me a talk on the geography of Merrion Street. Maybe,' said he, 'you would call down to number one Merrion Square and ask Sir William Wilde to come up and see me?' The poor man was in bits so I decided to go at once for Oscar's father. On the way down I had a look out for Joyce but I didn't see a bit of him. I knocked at number 1 Merrion Square and the door was opened by Sir William's wife Speranza. Before I could open my mouth, Speranza asked me for a word to rhyme with Indian meal and famine. 'This poem of mine must be in the *Nation* newspaper office before five o'clock or it won't get into the next edition,' said she.

'Can Oscar not help?' said I.

'No, Oscar's gone to hear Even'song in Christchurch Cathedral and Sir William's gone to find out where they got the idea to put his Celtic cross to the Four Masters in Berkeley Road. He had picked the spot outside Adam and Eve's Church at the corner of Rosemary Lane. After that, he's going to St. Mobhi's Churchyard with Dr. W. Stokes, W. F. Wakeman and George Petrie to search for Robert Emmet's grave. Now if it's a doctor you want, try number fourteen, Sir Philip Crampton.'

As I passed by number 11, I saw the brass nameplate, 'Dwyer Joyce'. Is he after changing his name I asked myself. Then I heard the singing of the 'Boys of Wexford' and I knew it must have been another Joyce. Now James himself was a fair singer but he didn't sing rebel songs. At number 14 I was nearly killed. Sir Philip wanted to know where his Moses, Bullrushes, his giant Onion and his bust was gone? 'For years,' he said, 'it stood at the corner of College Street right under the nose of the police station, and yet it was stolen. And I suppose,' said he, 'you heard about the night they got me out of bed to attend to an eminent gentleman that had fallen off his horse in College Green, and when I arrived in my pyjamas wasn't the eminent gentleman none other than the statue of King Billy himself. And now I hear that McHugh himself is gone as well and, you tell me that Surgeon Parke is lost in Merrion Square.'

'And so is James Joyce,' I added.

Sir Philip sent me at once to complain to Mother Ireland, who was sitting in Merrion Square park, that he hadn't heard her playing her harp all day. I went into the park and right enough Mother Ireland looked very sad. I sat down beside her, put my arm around her shoulder, gave her a bit of a squeeze and asked could I help her in any way. She looked at me and said, 'You and what Army son? To help me,' said she, 'you would want the Wall of China, and the Pyramids of Egypt wrapped in a ring around Merrion Square to keep the combine harvesters out. Them Children of Lir,' said she, 'stay out very late at night in Rutland Square.'

'I'll have to get Sybil to come up and see you,' said I,

'Rutland is gone for his tea, not only down the street but beside the Rotunda as well. It's now Parnell Square, called after Charles Stewart Parnell, the uncrowned King of Ireland.'

'Gawney Mack?' said Mother Ireland, 'I'll have to send for Grace O'Malley. That's it,'said she, 'put the women and youngwans in charge of Ireland, and give every man a "Finnegan's Wake".'

I suddenly noticed this little ould fella in a long black coat and bowler hat smiling in the background. 'Who are you?' I asked.

'I'm Mister Buttercrust Downes' said he. 'I put up the dough, or the bread as yez call it today, to give Mother Ireland her own bit of land in Dublin. If you take my advice,' he said, 'go over to Dan O'Connell, he lives in number fifty-eight.'

Well Dan was down in Tara and the maid said to try Sir Jonah Barrington at number 42. Jonah was gone to a duel in the Furry Glen in the Phoenix Park and they weren't sure whether he'd be back or not. The maid said to try Joe Sheridan Le Fanu at number 70. Well, Joe was too busy writing *The House by the Churchyard* and he even asked me to get him a copy of the *Evening Mail*. He was up to his eyes in ghosts, coffee and cigarettes and wanted to see if his letter to the Editor of the *Mail* was printed. 'I thought you were the Editor,' I said. He banged the door in my face, then he roared through the letterbox that Dr. Robert Graves lived in number 84 and he might be able to help me find Joyce and get Parke a compass.

The door of 84 was opened by Maud Gonne MacBride. 'Graves is out on a sick call,' said Maud, 'and Willie Yeats isn't getting back in here. Go up two doors to A.E. George Russell.' AE himself was in conference with the Gods and the Co-Op. Broken hearted, I got to the end of the Square. Three men were making their way to Ely Place. I thought I knew them so I let out a Dublin whistle. The three turned together. The first man was John Philpot Curran, who waves his wig and gown. The second man was George Moore, who said

139

hail and farewell. The third man was Oliver St. John Gogarty. Well, I wasn't going to ask about James Joyce. 'More swans on the Liffey, Mister Gogarty, and the address of that red-headed girl in Ringsend,' I said.

His answer was drowned out by the sound of horse's hoofs as a horseman galloped down from number 24 Merrion Street. The sudden roar of the word 'Hike, Hike, Hike,' and the scraping of the horse's shoes was something terrible. The horseman stopped his charger an inch from me beard. 'I'm Wellington, show me the way to Waterloo,' he said. I directed him out towards the mouth of the River Liffey and hoped the horse was a good swimmer. As soon as the horseman passed by, who do you think was coming up the Square arm in arm, only James Joyce and W. B. Yeats. 'Where's me quid, me boots, and me shirts?' said Joyce.

'And where's the spot where you and Nora met on Bloomsday?' I asked.

Well, down he brought me to Sir William Wilde's house. 'There,' said Joyce, pointing to a coal hole cover. 'That's the very spot. I had to move off it twice while I was waiting. First for the log man with a ton of pine logs, then for the coalman with two tons of White Haven Moss Bank Coal Balls.'

As I gave him the quid and promised to send him on the boots and the shirts, he told me that the Noblett's chocolates melted in his pocket while he was waiting for Nora. 'I brought her for a walk to Ringsend and I bought her tuppence worth of dates,' he said.

'Com'ere boy,' said I in me best Cork accent. In memory of his father like. 'Where do I send the boots and the shirts?' I asked.

'Oh,' he said, 'me new address is c/o Mr. W. B. Yeats, near the Tower in Sandymount.'

'I thought that Yeats was too old at forty years, for you to help,' said I. With that W. B. put in his spoke.

'Ah,' said he, 'all is changed utterly now, sure all Dubliners know that life begins at forty,' and him and Joyce headed for the 'Wind Jammer' in Lombard Street.

If yeh happen to see me in the Daisy or the Iveagh Markets searching for bargains in boots and shirts, don't say 'Janey Mack, look at yer man.' Say 'Gawney Mack' instead, and remember the gear is for Jemmy Joyce, Dubliner.

18

Down in the Alley O

THIS DUBLIN STREET folklore rhyme raises a few questions. What ships? What alley? Was it Crown Alley or Skippers Alley on the way to the Liffey River? Or was it Faddle Alley or Bull Alley on the way to the Poddle River? Maybe it was Thundercut Alley on the way to the Bradogue River in Broadstone. Yet it could have been Potters Alley on the way to the Tolka River or Glovers Alley on the way to the Swan River in Rathmines or Whitehorse Alley on the way to the Camac River at Bow Bridge. It was hardly the Ball Alley in Kildare Street on the way to the Dodder River at Ringsend. I suppose the clue is in the date 'the eighth day of November'. Well, I looked up the old Dublin annals for the month of November, and the nearest I came to great big ships was as follows. On the eighth day of November 1909 four great big battle ships of the Atlantic fleet under the command of H.R.H. Prince Louis of Battenbergh lands at Kingstown for a four day visit. The ships were open for inspection by Dublin's middle and upper-middle classes, but their visits took place and went by unheralded and unsung. The poor kids in the alleys of Dublin who had no chance whatsoever of a trip to Kingstown to see the great big ships, entered into their world of make-believe and brought the ships sailing through their own alley. They sang about it so much that their song became a way of life for Dubliners for over seventy years and it is still one of the top ten in many

142

The great big ships sail
Through the Alley O,
Through the Alley O,
Through the Alley O.
The great big ships sail
Through the Alley O
On the eighth day of November.

parts of the inner city and in the Liberties of Dublin.

During Christmas week me and my pal were looking at the huge selection of children's toys, Buck Rogers, Charlie's Angels, Superman, Spiderman, walkie talkies, robots, trains, Grand Prix racers and hundreds more.

'Paddy,' said I, 'we sure missed out as chisellers.' He looked at me and said, 'Do you know what I'm going to tell you, I wouldn't swop a good game of Relieve-e-o for the lot of them. That remark brought to mind another alley song.

Down in the Alley O,
Where we play Relieve-e-o,
Up comes her Mother O,
Have you seen me Katie O?
She's down in the Alley O,
Kissing all the fellas O.

Well, Relieve-e-o was mainly played with boys but now and again we let the girls join in, and somehow or another the game always ended up kissing the mots down in the alley. I think it was down in Rowerstown at the age of ten years that I got my first kiss during a game of Relieve-e-o. Alleys nowadays are very scarce; there were dozens of them in Thomas Street, High Street and Cornmarket. We still have the few in Meath Street and Francis Street. My three favourite alleys in Dublin are Copper Alley, Smock Alley and Engine Alley.

In Copper Alley in 1608 Lady Alice Fenton, widow of Sir Geoffrey Fenton, coined copper money. Lady Alice cleaned the copper with the pulp of rotten oranges. She had a contract with the Dublin dealers to keep her well supplied with rotten fruit. For the first twenty-seven years Lady Alice had no trouble getting a daily supply of rotten oranges, but in the year 1635 the new theatre in Werburgh Street opened. Now there was a demand for the rotten fruit, which instead of cleaning copper money was being pelted at actors and viceroys. Every time I walk down Mary's Abbey and see the rotten and damaged fruit I think what a shame it is that we haven't got Lady Alice with us still in Copper Alley. At the top of Copper Alley was the old entrance gate to Saul's Court Academy, the first Catholic School in Dublin after the suppression of the monasteries. Saul's Court, which was run by the Jesuit Society, was followed by Rosemary Lane School and Derby Square School where James Clarence Mangan learned to read and write. 'Oh! Mister Mangan,' the priest would say, 'you could be driving in your coach and four horses only for the drink.'

Copper Alley leads down into Lower Exchange Street. A funny name for Sráid Isolde. Everyone knows the opera 'Tristan and Isolde', but how many know that Isolde was the Princess of Dublin who gave her name to Chapelizod and that the ruin of her church still stands in Palmerstown? King Mark of Cornwall fancied Isolde, so he sent over Tristan to bring her over to Cornwall to be his Queen. On the boat across, one of the servants put love potions in Isolde's chicken and she and Tristan fell in love. Well, you don't do that on the King of Cornwall and get away with it. There was only blue bloody murder back in Cornwall; the King made a law that it was to be kept in the palace circle only, but someone 'blew the gaff' and the story began to make its rounds in the taverns of the three kingdoms and then of the world. The next thing was a twelfth-century poem entitled 'Roman de Tristan'; after that every cat, dog and devil was writing and illuminating the story of the Dublin Princess and her fella. They say that the best illuminated manuscripts of Tristan and Isolde are kept in the National Library of Austria. The story ended as King Mark was dying and he called out for Isolde to come and touch his wounds with the magic herbs from Ireland. But it was no good; the King was failing fast, poor Isolde was stricken by deep depression and she told King Mark that she would join him in death, after all wasn't she joined to him in wedlock all her life?

Copper Alley, Exchange Street and Essex Street West are on the site of the old Isolde's tower which was once part of the walls of old Dublin. Essex Street had many names in the past: Stable Alley, Cadogan's Alley, Smoke Alley, Orange

Street and Smock Alley. The name Smock Alley should never have been changed. The rere of St. Michael's and John's Church was the main entrance to the old Smock Alley Theatre. Here the acting and singing stars were adored in Dublin. The rotten fruit and empty bottles were reserved for the viceroy's box. Here you are in the footprints of Peg Woffington, Spranger Barry and the beautiful Gunnings.

For as long as I can remember the only two things that I read as a child in the newspapers were Mutt and Jeff and Inspector Wade and his assistant Donovan. Inspector Wade was better than the follyinupper and he came into the house every night except Sundays. I was twelve years of age when I began to read the headlines. The first headlines I read had a terrible effect on me. The big bold black letters spelt out the story title.

SACRILEGE – WOMAN GETS SIX YEARS IN JAIL

Before I read the story I remember saying to myself, 'Just imagine, I will be eighteen years of age before that woman gets out of jail.' In childhood time travels very very slowly and six years seemed an eternity. I read the story under the headline. The woman had committed a sacrilege in Meath Street Chapel; she didn't rob any money, she robbed the tabernacle. She took out the holy chalices and she scattered the sacred hosts along Engine Alley. The next day I was going for the bread to the Liberties and I went slowly down Engine Alley looking for sacred hosts among the gutter cobblestones. I didn't find any, and every time I went down the alley I looked for the sacred hosts. I never knew whether the alley was a holy place on account of the hosts or an evil place on account of the sacrilege. As the years went by I used to cycle down Engine Alley on my way to work; sometimes I prayed in Engine Alley for the poor woman in jail and other times I peddled fast trying to forget about the sacred hosts. Engine Alley always held me in a sort of spell. I had to pass it to take the shortest route, yet sometimes I found myself taking the long way round even when I was a bit late. I don't think I ever forgot the story of the sacrilege for a single day. In my early twenties I used to go to Mass in Meath Street Chapel on a Sunday. Looking at the tabernacle I used to think about the woman in jail for the six years and wondered where she was.

The priest who used to say Mass was the late Canon Gleeson. He was a powerful man and gave very lively, down-to-earth sermons. He was also a great speaker with a real loud voice. One Sunday he was giving a sermon about the finding of the Child Jesus in the temple. He started by saying, 'Well now it was like this. Every year the parents of Jesus used to go to Jerusalem for the Feast of the Passover. When Jesus was twelve years old they went up for the feast as usual. But when they were on their way home Jesus stayed behind in Jerusalem without his parents knowing. But look,' said Canon Gleeson, 'forget about Jerusalem. It was like this. Joseph, Mary and Jesus were coming down Thomas Street, Joseph turned into Meath Street and Mary went on down and turned into Francis Street and then into the Iveagh Market. Mary thought Jesus was with Joseph and Joseph thought the boy was with Mary. There they were, Joseph walking down Meath Street, and Mary walking down Francis Street. Well they both met at the Coombe and Jesus was lost. And where do you think Jesus was? Well, Jesus was in the temple among the doctors in Engine Alley.'

19

Holy James's Street and Jacobs

DUBLIN WIT IS SHARPEST in children. One only had to ask a simple question to get a witty answer. 'What's yer name?' got a million replies, like 'Butter and Krame', 'Johnny Mac Brown', 'Stab the Rasher', 'Lord Muck', and 'Clark Gable'. 'What's your address?' or 'Where do you hang out?' always got the answer, 'Dirty Lane' or 'Number one James's Street'. Johnny Mac Brown and Clark Gable were two of our fourpenny rush film heroes. Johnny Mac was the ageing, big porter bellied chap in the cowboy pictures. Johnny was about fifty years of age. In nearly all of his pictures his father got shot. His Da must have been ninety. 'Dad, Dad did they shoot you?' and poor Da lying on the floor and the room filled with gunsmoke. Then Johnny went out to get the gang that gave his Da the works. Johnny always talked to himself as he made his way to the old corral to saddle up his horse. He always got a rousing cheer. Of course after he got the crooks that shot his Da, he came back to find his Da sitting up in bed with a big bandage around his head and the Da smoking cigars and drinking whiskey. Johnny's Ma — she was about ninety too — was giving out to Da.

'Ye'll git yerself killed one of these days.'

'Shucks Ma,' Johnny would say. Da was all smiles even without his teeth. 'You're darn tootin' Ma.'

Then Johnny gave a big smile and a wave and rode off into the red sunset. We all came out of the picture house and

What's yer name?
Butter and Krame,
All the way
From Dirty Lane.

What's yer name?
Johnny Mac Brown,
Where do you hang out?
Number one James's Street.

I went to the pictures tomorrow
I took a front seat at the back
I fell from the stalls to the gallery
And broke the front bone of my back.

down the street went a thousand Johnny Mac Browns. 'Dad, Dad, I'll git them, Dad.' Sure it's no wonder that every kid's real name was Johnny Mac Brown.

Clark Gable was the good-looking film star. If anyone said to a girl that she was a horrible looking thing, she always answered by saying, 'You're no Clark Gable yourself'.

Dirty Lane is long gone now, replaced by Bridgefoot Street. But number one James's Street remains. Today it is the address of St. James's Hospital. In my childhood days it was the address of The South Dublin Union Workhouse. The Spike, the Paupers, the Unmarried Mothers, the abandoned babies, horror town between the two gates, one at Rialto and the other at number one James's Street. The old Dublin people used to say, 'I'd rather die in the gutter than end my days in the Spike'.

A poet once said, 'There's nothing sweet in the city except the lives of the poor'. If that be true then number one James's Street is the sweetest place in Ireland. The old workhouse was feared, avoided, and jeered, even the tram conductors called out the tram stage by stage, 'The Union now please, any more for the Union?'

One day a fellow upstairs with a few jars on him shouted back down to the conductor, 'There's four more up here'.

'Ah! It's not the Union for you me oul' flower,' said the conductor. 'Your stop is the Old Man's Home at Kilmainham Cross.'

Men who didn't want to curse or use the holy name in vain used the name of James's Street and Jacobs instead. In their angry moments they cried out 'Holy James's Street and Jacobs, will you get off my back?' Girls never cursed or used four-letter words, we as children used curses goodo. The best curser in Dublin was the Hairy Yank. But then we gave him plenty of training. The call 'Any dollars Yank?' brought forth a rain of curses that would shame Old Nick himself. 'Holy James's Street and Jacobs, will yis leave the poor man alone.'

The old street starting at number one above Mount Brown Hill and the forty steps and ending at Watling Street and Guinness's Brewery brings to mind many happy and sad memories of Dublin life and my early childhood years. Nearly fifty years ago the best shop in James's Street was The Kingdom Stores. One old penny could buy a big bag of broken biscuits. After school each day someone had a penny, so the dash was made to the Kingdom Stores. The bag of broken biscuits would feed ten kids and the owner of the bag would still have plenty left for himself. Holy James's Street and Jacobs, they were gorgeous. Jam Puffs, all the fancy swanky biscuits that our mothers could never buy, were devoured outside the Kingdom Stores. Sometimes the owner of the penny would not be a biscuit lover; in that case the penny was spent in Sean Fitzpatrick's on Jembo Balls, Lucky Balls, Woodbines, Black Liquorice Pipes, Fizz Bags or Sherbet Poweder and Jelly Spoons. 'Give us a lick of your jelly spoon, ah! go on, give us a lick.' There were no worries about germs spreading as a dozen tongues licked the jelly spoon filled with sherbet powder. The owner of the shop was the late Sean Fitzpatrick, the founder of the National Graves Association. Sean spent his lifetime dedicated to Ireland's Cause of Freedom and the perpetual care of the graves of our patriot dead. I always said that if Sean Fitzpatrick had been alive in the times of Robert Emmet, the grave of Emmet would never have been lost. A few doors down from the two shops was Ryan's Chemist. One of the Ryan's was in my class in school. Ryan's supplied free of charge dozens of rolls of Kodak film and developed them free as well. These films were all taken in Basin Lane School by our teacher Miss Gallagher. For these occasions I supplied the box type Brownie camera that my Ma got on Frys Cocoa coupons. Beyond Ryan's was O'Gorman's Pawn Office with its three brass balls. Meaning that two-to-one you won't get it back, we said.

'Don't spill any soup on your suit, Tom, or I'll be cut in the morning.'

'That's a lovely suit, is it Indigo blue?'

'Yes, in de goes on Monday and out de comes on Saturday.'

In a way the three brass balls represented the three queues

in James's Street, one queue for the Pawn Office, one queue for the tram, and one queue for the Fountain Picture Palace. Inside it was no palace! The flea house, the bowery, the woodeners and the rich smell of oranges, Jeyes' Fluid and piss. In the woodeners the free-for-all fighting, digging, pinching, throwing orange peels, pulling pig tails and kissing mots went on in every row. All through the pictures the usher flashed his flash lamp across our faces and belted us with his leather belt and roared at us to keep quiet. 'Shut up yous animals, shut up yous blackguards, shut up yous bowsies,' and the sweat rollind down his face. Just imagine paying fourpence to get your eyes blinded with light, the belt of a leather strap and insulted at the same time. Imagine calling us bowsies.

One of my pals had a Mickey Mouse watch, again thanks to Frys Cocoa coupons. Well, we were in the Fountain Picture Palace and we kept asking him what time is it. We didn't seem to see the two big red clocks on each side of the screen. 'What time is it?'

Out came the Mickey Mouse watch. 'It's three-thirty.'

'What time is it?' we asked again.

Out came Mickey again. 'It's four-thirty.'

'What time is it?'

Mickey's face shone in the dark. 'It's four-forty-five.'

'What time is it?'

Out it came, half of the black strap and no Mickey Mouse. Someone was after making love to the Mickey Mouse watch and used a razor blade to cut the strap. Well, the row that followed was nearly better than the pictures. The show stopped and the house lights went on and every kid in the woodeners was searched, but Mickey Mouse could not be found. 'Search the cushioners, search the cushioners,' everyone cried.

I suppose it was considered that anyone in the 'cushioners' was too grand to steal a Mickey Mouse watch. Anyway the 'cushioners' were never searched. The lights went out and the picture came on again, then the picture broke down. Everyone forgot the Mickey Mouse watch and started banging their

152

feet on the floor. 'Show the pictures, show the pictures.'

The screen lit up with a black and white circle, with numbers in the circle. Then came a black **XXX** then nine, eight, seven, six, and every kid was shouting out the numbers, 'Five', 'Four', 'Three', 'Two', 'One', and on came the picture to a roaring cheer. The cheer died down and there was no sound. 'Show the sound, show the sound, show the sound.'

The sound came on and everyone in the picture was going backwards. This was better than the Keystone Cops.

After the pictures we were all blamed on the Mickey Mouse watch being missing. 'I know yous didn't rob it,' said my pal, 'but why were yous asking the time so many times and two bloody big clocks on the wall?'

I suppose we were giving him a chance to show off. 'Ah, feck it,' said my pal. 'I told my Ma to get a watch with a chain on it.'

So off he went home to blame his poor Ma for not getting a chain on his Mickey Mouse watch. Holy James's Street and Jacobs, Mickey Mouse sure caused a fair bit of excitement in those far-off days.

I made my first Holy Communion in St. James's Church with the late Father O'Callaghan. In the May and June evenings I walked in procession all around Echlin Street and the Grand Canal Harbour and home again in my little white surplice and blue sash.

After Christmas every year we stood outside the Brewery gates begging tickets for the Guinness concert. 'Holy James's Street and Jacobs, have yous no tickets left Mister?' Mad Kevin didn't seem to want concert tickets, he held out his hand for pennies and thru'penny bits which he got by the dozen. The tickets were scarce and we never got any. The concert in those days was held in the Mansion House. It was the social event of the year with an all-star-studded cast. The kids used to boast about going to the concert and to add salt to our wounds they'd wave the blue, red or green tickets in our faces saying, 'How would you like to be me?' over and over again. Our only come-back was to sing:

How would you like to be me,
Up on an apple tree?
With a lump of jelly
Stuck in my belly.
How would you like to be me?

Well, if you think that before the concert was bad, after
the concert was brutal. We all got a blow-by-blow account of
the star-studded show, the free sweets, cake and minerals that
were given out to all the kids. Oh how we wished that we had
someone working in the brewery in holy James's Street.
Everyone working in Jacobs got free biscuits every week
and an Oxford Cake at Christmas. Real biscuits, none of your
broken ones like the Kingdom Stores muck. We always
defended the Kingdom Stores and said anyway you had to
break biscuits to eat them and what does it matter if the
Kingdom Stores breaks them for us. Besides free concerts,
Guinness's workers and their families had free doctors, free
bottles of medicine and free boxes of pills. And they hadn't
to queue like us in the dispensary on Emmet Road and
Steevens's Hospitals. And if you were really sick, Guinness's
doctor came out to see you in his motor car and got you a
bed in hospital. Sure, didn't Guinness's give radios to every
patient in Steevens's Hospital?

The street characters of James's Street were headed by
the Kings, Mad Kevin, the Cross Man, Hulla and the Bagpipes.
The Cross Man went into James's Street Chapel every Friday
at three o'clock. He took the big crucifix from the back of
the church and put it across his shoulders and carried it up
and down James's Street for about an hour. Then he put
it back in the chapel. Friday after Friday he repeated his
cross-carrying walks up and down 'Jamebow'. Hulla was a
local mongrel dog. He followed the Bagpipe Man all around
the pubs. As your man was playing his bagpipes, Hulla used
to sit beside him and sing. We never knew which noise was
the worst, Hulla or the Bagpipes. The Trumpet Man also
played in James's Street in the early afternoons, but his main
night stand was at Leonard's Corner and Clanbrassil Street.

Sometimes Hulla stopped singing to listen to the trumpet, but only for a few moments, he never deserted the bagpipes and seemed to prefer the green tartan sounds to the silver shining trumpet. If a talent scout had got Hulla and the Bagpipes on the Theatre Royal they would have become millionaires and film stars. Mad Kevin got free tram rides and free candles in James's Street Chapel. He lit dozens of them for everyone. He sure gave the candle-makers plenty of work.

As children we all drank in several pubs. It was the done thing in those days to go into a public house and ask the barman for a pint of water. 'A pint of water, please.' The barmen never refused. A big pint glass of clear ice-cool water was downed every day. One day at Hannon's Pub in James's Street a man asked us to leave him home to Mount Brown. He was footless. He used to say, 'Will one of yous get me, will one of yous get the eggs, will one of yous get my bike.' When we got him home, he gave us sixpence between three of us. Every Friday like clockwork we met him. He used to come down to Hannons for two dozen eggs. Hannons sold everything in the grocery and medical line as well as porter and whiskey. Old man Hannon used to wrap up every egg in a sheet of newspaper and pack it well in the egg box. While he was packing, your man asked for a pint. Well, the packing and the pints went on until the twenty-four eggs were all in the box and your man was langers. 'Will one of yous get me, will one of yous get the eggs and will one of yous get my bike.'

The 'Time gentlemen, please' clock hanging over Hannon's shelves is a beauty. In the words of James Joyce, it's gold by black by white with the name Anderson — Dublin, twenty-four inches in diameter. I suppose it was made by Michael Anderson, clock and watchmaker, 19 Parliament Street, Dublin.

The clock had many admirers including many film stars that came to perform in the Theatre Royal. They all said it was an antique worth a small fortune. Mister Hannon was very proud of his clock, his eggs and his drink. One evening, Burl Ives, the famous singing film star, was having a jar in

Hannon's when he spotted the clock. 'Would you sell me the clock?' said Burl.

'Well now,' said Mr. Hannon. 'You see, Mr. Ives, the clock goes with the house and if you care to make me an offer for both, I'll consider it.'

Burl was very disappointed. He only wanted the clock for over his dresser in his American kitchen in Hollywood. 'It sure would look good over my dresser,' said Burl. He made several pleas, he even took out his cheque book and told Mr. Hannon to name his price in dollars.

'Sorry, Mr. Ives, the clock and the house go together.'

'Well,' said Burl, 'has it any history?'

'This was a Fenian house,' said Mr. Hannon.

'No,' said Burl. 'I mean has the clock any history?'

'Oh! be God's, Oh, Holy James's Street and Jacobs,' said Mr. Hannon, the clock is steeped in history. Did you ever hear about the battle of Clontarf?'

'Yes,' said Burl. '1014 wasn't it, Good Friday, with King Brian Boru with a crucifix in one hand?'

'It was,' said old Man Hannon, 'and do you see that clock there?'

'I do' said Burl.

'Well,' said Mr. Hannon, 'King Brian Boru had the crucifix in one hand and that clock there on his other hand as a wrist-watch.'

'Holy James's Street and Jacobs,' said Burl.

The clock remained on the wall. Old Mr. Hannon went on to join King Brian Boru and I suppose to tell him that his watch was faring better than the Mickey Mouse watch that got knocked off in the Fountain Picture Palace. The house and the clock changed hands and now it is under the careful eyes of Mr. Peadar Brady, who at closing time every night smiles at its gold, black and white face and says, 'Time gentlemen, please.'

156

In memory and appreciation of the late Cathal Mac Garvey, composer, singer, wit and raconteur, who died the year I was born, 1927, I give you his great Dublin ballad 'The Green Line and the Little Yellow Rod', i.e. D.O.R.A., the Defence of the Realm Act.

The Green Line and the Little Yellow Rod

There's an artificial river flowing near Dedra Bridge,
There's a tram car runs across it to the town.
There's a broken down canal boat resting on a slimy ridge
And . . . the clock of Leech forever gazes down.

Of guttys, there were two, the Dedra people knew,
They were hotter than they felt inclined to tell,
And the scene of all their pranks were the Royal Canal banks
Though Mountjoy had witnessed some of them as well.
They were nicknamed 'Fox' and 'Cat' by the pals that with them sat,
On the bridge that spans the Royal's waters brown,
And though often on the rocks, the wily 'Cat' and 'Fox'
Could occasionally knock a trifle down.

This top-line double turn, Mick Maguire and Jamesy Byrne,
Were buttys since the days they mitched from school.
For years they'd searched for work from Rathfarnham to Clonturk
But, the danger of it dodged them as a rule.

Jamesy's build was round about, such was anything but stout,
Tho' in height he topped his butty by a span.
Lingering ever near a pub, they would seldom dream of grub,
Save their nightly *table d'hote* of 'wan and wan'.

Miss D.O.R.A. badly sat on the chancers 'Fox and Cat'.
At the time she closed all pubs at half past nine.
And she spoiled their chiefest plans from the 'Boot' to 'Nancy Hand'
And the pubs of Maher, Leech and McEntee.
With the jauntiest of jogs to walk out running dogs,
Whene'er the chance presented, they'd engage,
But they never farther went and their walking time was spent
In the shelter of the famous 'Cat and Cage'.

On an autumn evening bright, when the sun was at its height,
They sat together, much depressed in mind.
Buried deep in discontent, for they hadn't got a cent,
And they knew not where or how to raise the wind.
But their darksomeness grew bright, when a 'Johnnie' hovered in sight,
A fisher of the amateurish brand.
He was dainty, trim and neat, from his pale hair to his feet,
Lik: the up-to-date equipment in his hand.
As he gazed at them the while, Jamesy smiled a knowing smile,
Mick acquiesced 'That outfit ought to sell,
What do you think?' 'Blooming well.'
T'was a Green Line and a Little Yellow Rod.

It was brand new from the shop and a likely thing to 'pop'
And they swore as if before Great Justice Dodd,
T'was a half a dollar cinch and they pondered how to pinch
The Green Line and the Little Yellow Rod.
Soon a plan was formed, t'was Mick's, Jamesy said that he'd keep nix,
And the watcher's role, he started to assume.
As he moseyed round about, came to Jamesy's ear a shout.
Then a painful sort of sobbing through the gloom.

Mick returned in half an hour, running top speed twelve horse power,
Scarcely touching with his toes, the ground he trod.

He'd just breath enough to yell 'Beat it sharper than Blue Hell'
Here's the fellow with the Little Yellow Rod.'
As they sheltered in a lane, Jamesy asked him to explain.
How he-failed to get the rod he went to find.
Mick responded with a frown, 'I'm not able to sit down
For I got it, far too much of it, behind.
Now Jamesy shut your gob, t'was a bloomin' rotten job
To take that barefaced Johnnie for a Cod.
See my head all full of bumps and that gossoon made 'em lumps
With the butt end of his Little Yellow Rod.'

Now they're spitting thru'penny bits, where the Sons of Leisure sit
On the bridge that spans the Royal's water's brown.
They can scent the 'creamy jar', so near and yet so far,
And . . . the clock of Leech forever gazes down.